A NATURALIST'S EYE

A NATURALIST'S EYE

Twenty Somerset Years

Philip Radford

British Library Cataloguing-in-Publication Data

A CIP record for this book is available from the British Library

ISBN 978 0 902152 20 5

Design and printing by 4word Ltd, Bristol

Dedicated to my father, who loved nature

Only male Common Blues have blue on the wing; females are patterned brown, with orange spots round the wing borders. Favoured food plants are Rest Harrow and Bird's-foot Trefoil.

Contents

Acknowledgements

The author would like to thank Drs Pat and Dennis Hill-Cottingham for persuading him to turn these natural history essays into a book; members of the Somerset Archaeological and Natural History Society's publication committee for their support of the project; and Peter Ellis for his editing skill in bringing this book to publication.

A male Smew, a diving duck. Smews can be seen occasionally in winter on Somerset reservoirs; they have saw-bills – useful for holding slippery fish. Females are brownish, with a chestnut forehead and crown. The duck breeds in Northern Europe and Arctic tundra; Smews are very unlikely to be seen in England after March.

Introduction

Philip Radford stands in a line of remarkable British naturalists that goes back at least to Gilbert White of Selborne. This tradition is of the naturalist finding time from their ordinary work to act as recorder and historian of the natural history of their area. Philip's observations and records were made when he was a doctor in general practice when, for many years, he kept a keen eye on nature especially where he lives in the Quantocks, but also further afield in Somerset and across the county border into Devon. In retirement, of course, he has been able to devote much more time. His interests are primarily ornithological but he is also an expert on dragonflies and fungi, as well as keeping an eye open for all activity – not just what he knows about. His intimate knowledge of where to go to see nature in activity is demonstrated by the superb photographs which accompany this book, and by his wonderful recordings of bird song.

Philip belongs to that tradition of recording nature that has worked itself out over the years since Gilbert White into a commitment to county societies established in the nineteenth century, Philip's being the Somerset Archaeological and Natural History Society. Philip's principal contribution lies in the records and observations patiently collected and cross-checked that form an unparalleled body of knowledge across the county, and thence to the national bodies and so across the country as a whole. But this book comes from a different source. Almost twenty years ago, Philip started to write contributions to the Society's Newsletter, initially annually and then twice yearly. Just under thirty of these contributions are here. These are the relaxed thoughts and recollections of a naturalist looking back over each six-month or year period and setting out their highlights.

The reader will be struck by the impression that when Philip goes into the countryside of Somerset it comes to life. Birds behave in strange ways, whole spiders webs are consumed, stags fight for their territories while Magpies look for ticks on their backs, snakes eat frogs, Buzzards fly back to the nest with adders in their mouths, female toads are surrounded by male toads, birds join in creosoting, butterflies become drunk. Even when shopping in Taunton, Philip sees a rat swimming on the Tone through an unconcerned group of Mallards, or a Sparrowhawk pursuing its prey down the High Street. Philip seems to be always there when natural life occurs – the life that goes on without human involvement. But it cannot be the case that the wonderful descriptions in the following pages are of events that only take place when Philip is around. The truth is that it is there for all to see if only we had the eyes for it. If we, like all good naturalists, were able to have the patience to become invisible to other creatures then nature would come alive for all to see.

Philip obviously has this ability to wait and see. But by a stroke of good fortune it so happens that Philip also has the ability to make the whole scene come to life for us, the chairbound reader. He does it by a combination of exact description, interesting details, and a recognition of what is beautiful. There is also a frank admission of what remains unknown. Often an author goes out into the countryside and we feel they stand between us and it. They leave nothing to be said – no problems remain – and the countryside or the feature is just a static thing to be observed. Not so with Philip, he is the companion who says Look! and then we see. He makes us realise how much we must be missing on our walks. He tells us that bird behaviour is always full of surprises. He revels in the colours and the botanical details of mushrooms – so much so that we are almost with him on his return home, sharing that delicious Field Blewit supper. He brings dragonflies vividly before us. He is the perfect self-effacing guide. We might perhaps not be at his side waiting before dawn or standing still in freezing weather waiting for a Cetti's Warbler to make the next move, but we can share what it must be like in the following pages.

The photographs accompanying the text are a further illustration of Philip's approach to nature and his concern with both accuracy and beauty. Each image defines the creature, plant or mineral at a particular moment. These are not universally applicable records of a species such as one would find in the perfect photograph of the professional. In fact they are more involving than the carefully framed picture, and we find ourselves drawn in to the moment of the photograph in all its particularity.

We hope that the reader will find this book a source of great pleasure and interest. It carries with it the always important message for us at a time when instrumental views of nature prevail – that life in nature is going on regardless of us or our needs, and that its importance lies simply in its being there.

Peter Ellis, Honorary Editor
Somerset Archaeology and Natural History

Ducks, Waders and other birds at Steart;
an Avocet and a Grey Plover; how waders feed; the beauty of Lapwings and their names; Curlews, Dunlins and Oystercatchers. Spring 1988 and winter 1989

After passing Otterhampton church, the road from Cannington leads across fertile green fields to reach the muddy shore of the Bristol Channel at Steart. There is something distinctive about the waves of the shore here – so much muddy silt gives them a brown colouring which is not often seen elsewhere in Britain. Sadly, the beach is littered with rubbish of all dimensions, much of it plastic, but this is the place to see large numbers of sea and shore birds.

Especially beautiful were flocks of resting Shelduck on the sands; these largely black-and-white ducks, with rich chestnut patches on the body and greenish heads, are certainly frequent in Bridgwater Bay. As so many Shelduck moult in autumn in the area, it is perhaps to be expected that a large number remain throughout the winter. It was thrilling to discover a single Avocet which was feeding in the shallows of the incoming tide. The slim, white, black-lined wader moved its remarkable up-curved bill from side to side in the water, so obtaining its food particles in its own specialised manner. Another wader, watched feeding in shallow pool water, was a solitary Grey Plover; here, using its short black bill, edible items were picked delicately from the surface or from the nearby salt-marsh. Of finches, numerous Greenfinches were searching for weed seeds in local vegetation. Some House Sparrows and Chaffinches were mixed in these parties and, in addition, one Yellowhammer was noted. Small flocks of Skylarks fed in the inland fields and a few Meadow Pipits were sighted as well. However, probably the most spectacular of the small birds seen was a cock Stonechat, showing its black head and white collar from the top of a fence post.

More than a year later I walked along the shore at Steart on a December day when the Somerset and Welsh hills were capped with snow and a penetrating, gusty wind drove from the north. High tide was at 11 am, so, as this approached, birds were displaced from their tidal mud feeding areas to the beach or inland pasture fields. Shelduck were again present in big numbers. Many were tossing on cold, silt-laden waves in the Channel, all facing into the wind. Others were squatting on shingle, seemingly massed together; even so, it could be seen that there was a discrete minimal distance between each duck. Dotted between the Shelducks were black, upright Cormorants; each bird was motionless and evidently replete with fish. Some twenty or so Grey Plovers dozed on the shore; short black bills and wings speckled with black and a general broad appearance suggested the identification. It was confirmed when one bird raised a wing, showing a black patch close to the pale body; for this reason, it could not have been a Golden Plover. Each Grey Plover, very sensibly, was in shelter behind a grass tuft. Birds-of-prey were not well represented on this occasion, except for a distant Kestrel. I was pleasantly surprised by a covey of Grey Partridges which rose from a grassy ditch and made off with whirring wings. The rounded, short wings, with a rufous tint to the head and tail proved the identification; moreover, there was no white neck and throat patch as with the somewhat similar Red-legged Partridge.

By far the commonest small bird present was the Greenfinch. A flock of about a hundred ranged around the reed-beds and many searched the shore verge for weed seeds. Chaffinches were feeding as well, but not in large numbers. Curiously, a single Goldfinch rose from a nettle bed to rest in a wind-blown elder bush. Amongst buntings, a lone female Reed Bunting was seen to fly across a clearing among the reeds. One unexpected wader which was identified was a Wood Sandpiper, which rose showing its white tail and rump. This bird could not have been a Green Sandpiper as this species has very black wings, both above and below, and the white rump patch is large and conspicuous.

Large numbers of Lapwings were in the area and it was a delight to watch these round-winged waders, either flying separately or in compact flocks. But it is when an individual bird is scanned through binoculars that its real beauty is realised. The dark green of the wings glints to a purple reflection in sunlight and the long wisp of a crest ensures that there can be no confusion with any other shore bird. Lapwings' calls give character and atmosphere to any field, marsh or estuary. Various intonations of 'pee-wheet' are uttered, with different emphasis in social and contact calling. Of course, the Lapwing's country name of 'Peewit' represents an onomatopoeic form of the cry. The call seems so appropriate for a wheeling green wader, conspicuous with a black band at the end of its broad, white tail as it dives and tumbles overhead. It is known that Lapwings have decreased as breeding birds in many parts of England and Wales in recent years although numbers have been maintained in Scotland. Without ringing evidence, it was impossible to be certain whether the Lapwings I was observing had originated in Scotland or in Scandinavia; nevertheless, a big population certainly winters along the shores of the Bristol Channel. When on the ground, the Lapwings were either resting peacefully in the face of the icy wind or seeking food. If feeding, a Lapwing would run a short distance and, after a pause, would bend forwards to peck or probe into the mud. Lapwings have short bills so the food they seek must be near the surface; small invertebrates, such as ragworms, bristle-worms or shrimps were probably taken from the tidal mud. When feeding on the inland fields, earthworms were doubtless the Lapwings' prey items.

Another conspicuous, large wader feeding on the shore and often drawing attention by its bubbling, musical cries, was the Curlew – readily told in flight by its white rump patch. Curlews are common as winter visitors in the Bristol Channel zone, obviously benefiting by the large tidal movements and the exposure of so much mud. The wader's name indicates its wild and far-carrying cry; probably it is the male which sings and almost dances on its moorland breeding haunts, but both sexes appear to call when in social contact. Curlews have long, curved bills, with those of the females having greater lengths than those of the males. Thus, for deep prey, the female has the advantage over the male, which must be a help when feeding up for egg-laying, particularly during cold spring weather conditions. It was noted that plenty of Curlews were feeding on the farmland fields, especially when the tide was at its height; like Lapwings, they were, no doubt, seeking earthworms. On the mudflats, mussels and cockles are known to be eaten as well as crabs and ragworms.

With normal winter temperatures, Dunlins have abundant food supplies in the Bristol Channel inter-tidal zones. Dunlins extract food items, mainly small molluscs, worms or shrimps, by mud probing; the bill is a relatively long one for so small a wader and is slightly down-curved. Some Dunlins breed in Britain, including Dartmoor, but Scotland holds most of the nesting pairs for these islands. Interestingly, a local name for the bird in Scotland is 'Plover's Page', because it may be seen with the Golden Plover. In this company, a Dunlin can concentrate on feeding, apparently knowing that a nearby Golden Plover will give ample warning of the approach of danger. When the hen Dunlin lays her clutch of four eggs in summer, the total egg weight represents about seventy per cent of her total body weight. Hence it is vital that the female Dunlin has access to rich feeding grounds while laying; this is normally available on the Arctic tundra in summer, with vast numbers of crane-fly and midge larvae being present in the soil and pools.

Larger molluscs are the usual food items for Oystercatchers which were common along the shore and betrayed by their occasional musical pipings. Oystercatchers open mussels either by cutting shell-holding muscles or rupturing the shell by hammering with their chisel-like beaks; in addition, they hunt for cockles. One Oystercatcher may eat two to three hundred cockles per day, so these attractive black-and-white waders with red legs and bills are not always popular with local people. As with all shore waders, the time of feeding depends on exposure of mud, and thus the food source, by the outgoing tide. Many waders will feed at night, particularly with a full moon; after all, most food items are located by touch. It is interesting to know that about half of Europe's wading birds feed in winter on British tidal estuaries.[1]

1 An Oystercatcher's nest and eggs, sometimes found along the Somerset shore. The birds' penetrating and piping calls are commonly heard near the coast in winter, although not so frequently in summer; these four well-camouflaged eggs will take some covering by the brooding bird. Hopefully, the clutch will not be smashed by a careless walker or discovered by a roving Red Fox or vigilant Carrion Crow!

Feeding and predating birds; *Thrush and Fieldfare fights in the snow; spawning frogs; nest clutch numbers. Early 1990*

How well birds feed must depend on weather conditions. Unduly cold spells alter the availability of food items, either by covering vegetation with snow and ice or by freezing which prevents insect hatching. There were many examples of these factors at work in Somerset in the early months of 1990. Around New Year Siskin parties were feeding in luxury on alder seeds on trees in the Quantock valleys. In the oak woods, visiting Woodcocks were also plump and well nourished, as could be seen when they rose from their concealment in the leaf litter, usually well before one was aware of their presence.

In February came the snow and Sparrowhawks snatched birds from gardens where they had come for easy meals. Resident birds became enemies as they squabbled over scraps: I recall several fights between possessive Mistle Thrushes and also between Fieldfares; fallen apples were commonly the lure and a bird would repeatedly pin an enemy on its back in the snow and leave all kinds of wing and feather impressions. In particular, Mistle Thrushes, with raised wings and tails spread in aggression, would fly at each other and then tower upwards for several feet before one would slink off in defeat. Meanwhile, smaller birds became simple prey for eager, prowling cats, foxes and vigilant birds-of-prey, including hungry Kestrels which normally prefer a diet of voles. Some birds took advantage of the abundant beech seeds which were lying in the woods after last autumn's bumper crop. Chaffinches fared well on beech nuts as well as ground-feeding Great Tits. On one occasion I saw a wintering hen Blackcap taking beech seed from the forest floor in company with Great Tits; clearly, as no insects would be available a bird such as a Blackcap must adapt to eating seeds or berries. After the snow, Long-tailed Tits were depleted in numbers on the Quantock Hills and so it was with Wrens and Robins. Rooks lost no time in stick-carrying and building their bulky, exposed tree nests. With so much cawing, as well as stick dropping and stealing, rookeries are noisy places even in mid-February. The sturdy Rooks usually have eggs in their nests by early March while the hardier and larger neighbouring Ravens have often laid by mid-February.

By early March the local Common Frogs were spawning, with males croaking intermittently through the night and sometimes by day, although occasional icing over of the ponds did interrupt the process.[2] Several hibernating butterflies were seen on the wing when it was sunny on those late-winter days, notably Brimstones and Peacocks. About this time, I noted a male Blackcap in good song; of course, it was impossible

2 A Common Frog, evidently a male, looking out for a willing mate at a breeding pond in spring. Common Frogs are very variable in colour; they are the most widespread frog species in Europe. Breeding seems to be getting earlier in Somerset with spawn sometimes appearing in January; whether such spawn will survive, however, must depend on weather conditions.

to say whether this was an early spring migrant from Africa, or, if it was a winterer which had been born in Scandinavia and was destined to return there.

I saw my first 1990 Swallow in flight near Bicknoller on the first day of April. As Swallows feed on insects taken on the wing, their food intake during so chill an April must have been very low. Indeed, numbers of Swallows and House Martins have been scanty in Somerset throughout the spring and early summer, with arrival dates in many areas being delayed generally. Yet Cuckoos, feeding on caterpillars, appeared to arrive on time in April on Exmoor and in the Quantocks region. Quite unexpectedly, an unusual bird, which is usually a late migrant to England, was present and in song near Shapwick in late May. Thanks to information from a friend, I heard the melodious and imitative song of a Marsh Warbler in dense bog vegetation, and at the same time, the loud medley of notes from an unseen Cetti's Warbler. I expect the Cetti's Warbler was a resident, but Marsh Warblers spend their summer on the Warwickshire Avon and by the Severn – at least, that used to be so.

Swifts were delayed as well as Swallows and with the dry, cool May and showery June the flying insect population has been low. In consequence, the breeding success of the Somerset Swifts has been poor. In early July I saw many Swift parties behaving as though early southerly migration had already started. Because of the chilly May weather, I expected warbler nesting to be delayed and egg numbers to be small. However, Willow Warbler nests I have seen have had full clutches of six eggs and it was the same with breeding Wood Warblers. Blackcaps too have had five eggs in the nest, where I thought there would be just three or four. With warblers, I think there was some nesting delay in May; even so, by June there was plenty of rain with higher temperatures so there was a good supply of local invertebrate food. With quick grass and leaf growth, nests became well concealed.[3] The nestlings in the warbler nests I observed grew well and flew successfully although I know that, in some cases, young died from cold and dampness. The dull, showery June weather has not encouraged butterflies to fly and mate and the same applies to dragonflies.

3 A nest of eager young Wood Warblers on the woodland floor, soon to leave to face the outside world. I wonder if any of them will succeed in returning to the Quantock Hills next spring, following a winter spent in Africa, and with air travel each way?

Fungi, edible, hallucinatory and poisonous; what happens to the slugs who eat Death Cap fungi?; the perfect blue of Sheep's-bit; damselflies and deer. Later 1991

In late September I searched for fungi on the Quantock Hills. As August and September were so dry, the number of fungal species located was not great although the search was most enjoyable. A fine specimen of the Hedgehog Fungus was discovered, showing the down-pointing spines on the under-surface of the white, bulky cap. Hedgehog Fungi are edible and of fine flavour; unfortunately, they are not common in Somerset. Other edible fungi found came from the Boletus group; here the agaric has pores instead of gills, which one might expect, under the cap. One handsome specimen found was a birch-associated Bolete, with a truly orange-coloured cap. During October I came across a big group of Liberty Caps on a grassy place on Exmoor (the Somerset part, naturally). These little white agarics, with their pointed, attractive caps, are well-known because they contain a chemical which will hallucinate – that is, give rise to false sensations. Some people have had hallucinatory parties using these fungi; after eating twenty or thirty of these small fungi a person may be confident of flying from an upper window – such is the dangerous property of the poison. I wonder if deer, rabbits or squirrels eat these fungi and, if so, what is the effect?

Then, at the end of October, I saw another fungal species which has even more deadly chemical power. In a glade near oaks on the Quantocks there was a slug-eaten capped fungus with a yellow-green, slimy top with hanging, paper-like pieces of membrane at the edges and at the upper part of the stalk; like the membrane, the gills were white. Two other fungi were present of the same species and both were again well eaten by slugs. This was the Death Cap; one agaric is enough to kill a man and it is poisonous in all parts of its structure: the poisoning process is usually a delayed one. One feels the significance of the occasion when handling a Death Cap, yet slugs seem to thrive on them. I have looked for dead slugs in the herbage near Death Caps but I have found none so far. The ability of certain plants to consistently elaborate complex poisonous chemicals is remarkable; equally, it is remarkable that some animals can detoxicate such chemicals while others are affected fatally. One small, delicate white fungus, which has been very common in Somerset this autumn, has been one of the white funnel caps, growing readily on lawns and by roadsides. Again, this species is poisonous. The top of the cap shows concentric rings and the gills are swept down the stalk, giving the agaric a rather lovely architecture. Nevertheless, some householders may not be aware of the poisonous nature of the innocent-looking white fungi in their garden.

Near the site of the Exmoor Liberty Caps I discovered the bright but
late flowering Sheep's-bit; surely one of the most beautiful blues in
nature. These flowers were conspicuous near Pinkworthy Pond where
interest is added by dragonflies which are usually in flight in summer
over the water and nearby. The Common Hawker flew over the acidic
moorland, which is its normal habitat, and plenty of Black Darters were
seen too; also, the pond verges held a good population of Emerald
Damselflies. The Emerald Damselflies flew near Common Sundew plants
which live by catching insects; happily I did not see any ensnared
damselflies!**[4] [5]**

I watched Red Deer on the Quantocks in October, when the stags
guard and maintain their hind herds. Belling gives evidence of the
presence of a possessive stag, especially at night, in the darkness. The
older stags, with several points to their antlers, appear to get most hinds
– due, I suppose, to both strength and experience. Younger stags get
their chance of a hind herd later in the autumn, when their seniors have

4 This Common Sundew, occasional on the Somerset Levels and marshy parts of Exmoor, is a plant to be
wary of if you are a fly or a small damselfly. The digested insect gives the plant nitrogen which is lacking in
the soil.

5 Emerald Damselflies are found by well-vegetated ditches and pond margins; here, a male has seized a female by the neck to form a tandem pair and they will shortly fly off for egg-laying. With this species, eggs are inserted into the stems of water vegetation such as rushes or reeds; the male is on guard while the female does the work.

6 A herd of Red Deer hinds near Triscombe in summer. In autumn, roving stags will collect as many hinds as possible into harems in preparation for the rutting season. A powerful stag, with its formidable antlers, will guard its hinds by roaring and by charging at any intruder. Large stags will sometimes collect over thirty females; after the rut, which will last about two weeks, the hinds disperse and the exhausted stags will move off elsewhere.

had their will. Occasionally herds in autumn have more than one young male; on Exmoor in mid-October I observed a herd of fourteen Red Deer which included three stags of adolescent type – commonly called prickets, I believe. As winter advances, so the Red Deer move from two sex to one sex herds; perhaps it is as well that human beings do not behave in similar manner!**[6]**

Woods and reservoirs; *a Sparrowhawk stoops in a gale; carrion eating birds; the perils of female toads; toads and butterflies. Earlier 1992*

Many Somerset woods in December are characterised by their population of noisy, squeaky Pheasants, where the numbers have largely been artificially boosted. Also noisy, however, are the similarly introduced Guineafowl. At dusk the birds group together in pleasing, murmuring assemblies on the ground before they flutter in succession to their chosen roosting branches. Seemingly, they whisper and converse together before dozing off, but any disturbance will provoke them into a protesting clamour: both Guineafowl and Pheasant give warning of danger to each other. Certainly winter walks in the Quantock woods are enlivened by the game birds but I prefer to hear the sounds of Buzzards as they circle overhead and male Mistle Thrushes experimenting with their early territorial springtime songs.[7] Visiting Goldcrests may infiltrate locally and by December on the Quantock Hills the oak woods normally contain a satisfying number of Woodcocks which rest by day while near-invisible in the leaf litter; nearby, a Red Deer stag or hind may be lying, also well camouflaged in a collapsed mass of dead Bracken. The forest oaks and beeches are bare in December but where there are clearings and a few conifers, so a Sparrowhawk is likely to be seen. The speed of a Sparrowhawk's swoop across a glade to seize a lingering Chaffinch or Great Tit is an event to make any country walk memorable.

   Somerset's reservoirs are worth visiting during winter and a recent feature has been the increasing numbers of Cormorants. No doubt the Cormorants, like Grey Herons, find good fishing at the reservoirs; I feel they are particularly spectacular as they stand black, bulky, sombre and well fed while drying outstretched wings. Tufted Duck, Pochard and Mallard are frequent on the reservoirs and maintain good numbers until spring, providing that the waters are not iced over. Then Coot, Moorhen, Little and Great Crested Grebe, which often breed locally, give variety in appearance and vocalizations – there is variety in methods of feeding too.[8] Last December and January Somerset held vast numbers of Black-headed Gulls and surely one of the best places to view these raucous birds is in Taunton by the River Tone, where they compete with ducks for bread thrown by kindly people. The gulls are in their winter plumage by this time but the occasional one has at least a partial brown hood: one wonders if it is either a precocious individual or one with a delayed moulting mechanism. There can be other surprises also when looking at Black-headed Gulls, for amongst a flock last winter, over the River Tone, I saw a bird with a thin, black bill and a black edge to the

7 This is a young Buzzard of the year, photographed at dawn at its roosting site in late August. Buzzards have certainly increased in numbers in Somerset in recent years and several may be seen soaring together in spring display flights; a common sight now is a Buzzard waiting patiently on a branch for a Rabbit to appear. Buzzards used to be called 'Great Rabbit Hawks', so they fare badly if myxomatosis reduces the Rabbit population; even so, the birds are very partial to earthworms on ploughland. The mewing calls of Buzzards, their frequent mobbing by Carrion Crows in summer, and the occasional glimpse of one of their big stick nests in a tree in a local copse, all combine to be part of Somerset bird life these days.

back of the wing: I concluded that this must be a Bonaparte's Gull, which is a North American species.

During a December gale I happened to surprise a female Sparrowhawk as she stooped at a Blue Tit. The hawk veered to fly directly into the full force of the wind; in spite of the gale's power, the hawk did not appear impeded in any way. The December temperatures were relatively warm and one day I noticed a small bat, species unknown, in a to-and-fro flight near trees during the afternoon. More remarkably, a friend told me that he had noted two House Martins flying at Crewkerne in the same month. In the New Year, Ravens honked increasingly loudly over the Quantock Hills; a pair would soar and circle before the two birds flew at speed towards each other, only to separate again. Apart from mating displays, the Ravens seek carrion and will also attack sickly or dying lambs or injured rabbits; they have a reputation too for pecking at the eyes of helpless animals. Of course, Ravens breed early, by February eggs

8 Great Crested Grebes, once so scarce because of the demand for their head plumes for use in the millinery trade, are not uncommon as breeding birds on Somerset lakes and reservoirs, providing there is plenty of vegetation round the edges. In spring, the sight, and sound, of displaying birds on the water, with head shaking and spread neck ruffs, is memorable; later, there is the added attraction of watching young grebes being carried on the backs of their swimming parents. Nests are usually floating, or partially so, with eggs being covered with water weeds as the sitting bird slips off the nest for a feed.

have often been laid in a new or an old big stick nest. Happily there was nesting success for the Quantock Ravens during the season.

In February I noticed a Song Thrush digging by a hedge and pulling out and swallowing pieces of the roots of Cuckoo-pint. Later, in my garden, a cock Pheasant was watched excavating by the large, cultivated Cuckoo-pint plant; again, root portions were eaten. This annoying behaviour by the Pheasant continued over several weeks, leaving really large holes in the flower-borders. About the same time, and without annoyance to the land-owner, some hundreds of Chaffinches fed on farm fields in the region of the Quantocks: the numbers of these attractive birds seemed bigger than is usual. In February and in March vocal and mating Common Frogs were reported from all over Somerset and, subsequently, it was the same with Common Toads. Near Stogumber I noted some dead frogs with their abdomens ripped open with the intestines apparently eaten; I wondered if this was the work of Tawny Owls by night or if Carrion Crows were the culprits by day. Then, on a pond on the Quantocks in mid-March, I saw a seething raft of eight to ten Toads; in the centre was a pathetic female, being grasped by over-eager, competitive males. One could only assume that female Toads were in short supply. Inland in Somerset in April, Siskins were common, feeding in alders and in conifers and, as expected, bird song increased and migrants began to appear. Chiffchaffs were singing generally in Somerset by late March and I heard a Blackcap in good melody in early April, yet Swallows were late and I did not see one over the Quantocks until mid April. By the end of the month Cuckoos were calling well and the females gave their distinctive hinny-type phrases, especially on the moorlands.

There is always a thrill on listening to the first Wood Warbler song of the year and a greater delight on seeing a pair in display; this May I was fortunate to watch the building of two nests and, in all, I had three under observation.**[9]** Two nests had six eggs and the remaining one contained seven; these all hatched to give a total of nineteen nestling Wood Warblers. Surprisingly, considering their numerous enemies, all flew from their nests; I wonder how many eventually set out on their migratory journeys to Africa?

Considering the warm, fine weather conditions of May and June, the number of butterflies, in general, was low at first but later this improved.

9 The nest of a Wood Warbler with a clutch of seven eggs, photographed in May in a Quantocks wood. With seven eggs, the female was evidently well nourished, but eight eggs have been recorded. Wood Warblers nest in closed-canopy woodland, with the domed nest being built on the forest floor, usually very well concealed. The nest looks like that of a Willow Warbler but, in contrast, no feathers are used for the lining which is prepared from very fine dried grasses.

10 A male Broad-bodied Chaser showing its handsome pruinose blue body and brown patches at the wing bases; females have yellow bodies, perhaps looking rather like Hornets. Males fight a lot, so the blue pruinose bloom often gets eroded in places. As mating usually occurs only during flight and is very brief, I fear that I will never succeed in getting a photograph of the event!

11 The Emperor is the largest British dragonfly; the male, blue with a distinctive black line down the centre of the back, has a long flight season, extending from early June until well into August. This photograph was taken near West Quantoxhead in July; as the Emperor is a tireless flier opportunities for photography are strictly limited. Emperors will fly after large insect prey, often taking butterflies.

Clouded Yellows have been sighted this summer; so far I have noted six: two in Devon, two on the Mendips and two on the Quantocks. With dragonflies, many Banded and Beautiful Demoiselles were in sunny flight over the upper parts of the River Tone in early summer. Four-spotted Chaser dragonflies have been frequent and the very colourful Emperor Dragonfly, a tireless flier (frustratingly so for a photographer) has had a long season on the wing.**[10] [11]**

A Blackbird's reflection; *value of teeth and claws in feeding; bird mating and bird nests; dragonflies on Mendip; a Green Woodpecker swallows a spider's web whole. Earlier 1993*

Around last Christmas a female Blackbird started to tap vigorously at the sliding glass sun-roof of my car, when parked in my car-port. The noise drew my attention to the bird but, when chased off, she returned to the attack within a minute or two; indeed, I do not know how the Blackbird found time to eat at all during those short winter days. But the attacks continued, with considerable fouling of the car roof: they could only be stopped by parking the car elsewhere or putting a drape on the roof. It is well-known that territorially minded birds will readily attack their reflections on glass – or even ice. Usually it is the aggressive male which attacks; commonly this involves Pied Wagtail, House Sparrow, Blue or Great Tit, Robin or Carrion Crow. I do not know why my garden hen Blackbird, in mid-winter, was so determined to lunge at her reflection on a horizontal surface, rather than the commoner vertical one.

Recently, I was reminded that some animals eat very well without the use of teeth. One morning I saw a female Sparrowhawk perched on a post in pouring rain, where it remained patiently for fully two minutes. Suddenly the hawk flew at speed into a conifer, dislodging some eight hiding Blue, Coal and Great Tits. Using a talon, the Sparrowhawk grasped a tit which was carried off to be plucked and its ribboned flesh eaten; here, a hooked beak was the very adequate tool and no teeth were present or even required.

No teeth were needed either to grasp the gist of a discussion between fellow naturalists on dowsing and water divining. I have seen demonstrations carried out but it seems that no adequate scientific explanation can be offered to account for the real powers of some people. Probably, complex electro-magnetic forces are concerned; I suspect that the subject will remain a nebulous one for many years yet.

In March, however, the signs of the coming spring were far from being nebulous as Small Tortoiseshell and Brimstone butterflies flew in welcome sunshine. Blackbirds and Song Thrushes carried nesting materials and Quantock Ravens croaked and yapped in their contact calls, while carrying carrion to their already hatched young. In late March, Chiffchaffs were in full song, having returned from migration, and Long-tailed Tits carried feathers in their beaks to line their warm, mossy and lichened nests. As expected, Cuckoos appeared over the Quantocks in the middle of April. I was impressed how one male, which perched on a moorland hawthorn, was quickly mobbed by four or five Meadow Pipits, which appeared as if from nowhere. Clearly, Cuckoos with their hawk-like appearances are not popular amongst small breeding birds and mobbing can be predicted: little peace and rest is allowed. Yet some behaviour among birds cannot be predicted; for instance, in May I saw a male Stonechat, after hovering, descend to make pattering movements with its feet on soft earth near a stream. Black-headed Gulls or Ringed Plovers will patter on wet sand or soil, attempting to lure worm prey to the surface but I have never seen a Stonechat act in this way previously – even though it attracted no prey on this occasion. There were no pattering birds on a May walk along the River Barle near Tarr Steps and, sadly, sightings of both Dipper and Grey Wagtail were negative. However, caddis-fly and mayfly larvae were frequent and a fresh-water limpet was discovered. Several birds were feeding their young and good views were available of both Nuthatch and Treecreeper visiting their woodland nests. Various fern species and colourful flowers, such as Pink Purslane, were examined.

It is always a pleasure to watch the mating display of any bird and, for me, this is especially so for the Wood Warbler, particularly if subsequent nest building and the growth of the young to the flying stage can be observed.[12] This summer I watched two such Wood Warbler pairs and I was interested how the amount of territorial songs, and contact calling,

12 A Wood Warbler leaving the nest after feeding the brood. Nests are built in May in recesses on the forest floor; they are often on a slope and rapidly growing grass will conceal the entrance after building.

13 Meadow Pipit nestlings photographed in June: when is the next caterpillar going to arrive? Note the down which covers the chicks and gives excellent insulation until feathers are grown. Meadow Pipits are common birds of moorland.

varied between the individuals. One Wood Warbler I observed was clearly unmated; it sang almost throughout the day in May and early June but no mate was attracted and so no nest was built. For those who like to listen to the territorial songs of birds, Wrens can be most annoying. Their loud, penetrating songs so often intrude, swamp and overwhelm the more delicate and subtle cadences of other birds, in spite of the Wren's small size. In early June, I was listening to a mix of warbler song in a woodland glade when a Wren appeared and flitted about in bracken vegetation just a metre or so before me. I expected the usual high-amplitude interruption but, instead, the bird remained mute. Soon I realised that the Wren was a female; moreover, she was waiting nervously to enter a nest concealed in dead bracken which I had not spotted earlier. Hastily, I retreated, leaving the Wren to add another egg to her incomplete clutch; subsequently, I was rewarded by the sight of well-grown young food-begging at the nest aperture. At the time, I was intrigued to see the visiting female parent search the ground below the nest for dropped faecal sacs; these were carried off, as were any actually deposited in the nest. This behaviour must have survival value for the species, although the male parent Wren did not seem to bother over such details.

   Following rainy spells, there was sunshine for a walk to look at dragonflies on the Mendip Hills in July. Several spectacular Emperor Dragonflies were on the wing and a Four-spotted Libellula alighted to eat its meal of a male Azure Damselfly – so providing an excellent photographic opportunity. In addition, a Common Blue Damselfly was noted trapped by a spider's web, no doubt awaiting ingestion by a hungry, possessive owner. Local plants were observed as well as dragonflies; the nature of Purple Moor-grass, with its tall tussocks, was certainly demonstrated when walking over a particular boggy section of the moor! Returning to the webs of spiders, I was surprised to see a juvenile Green Woodpecker fly at a large orb-web on a tree near Quantock woodland. Using its long tongue and opening and closing its bill, the entire web, together with trapped insects, was swallowed. For birds, the investigation of spiders' webs must yield many helpless, ensnared insects, just there for the taking. Also on the Quantock Hills, in July, I was surprised to see a male Blackcap pulling apart the flowers of Marsh Thistle and eating the achenes (or fruits) of the pappus; of course, in summer, Blackcaps normally live on insect food. From the agile behaviour of the bird on the Marsh Thistle plants I though at first that the black-capped bird was a Marsh Tit; however, there was no doubt at all regarding the true identification. When watching birds, it is so often the unexpected which happens.[13]

Attracting moths at night; *more fungi; a Harvest Mouse's nest; a headless Southern Hawker; the autumn rut. Later 1993*

August was not a wet month in the Quantock area of Somerset although on one day 23.9mm of rain fell compared to the average per day on my rain gauge of 1.23mm. However, there was no rain when I walked near Greenaleigh Farm beyond Minehead looking at the sandstone cliffs. Using a hand lens, rock fragments were scanned for grain size, but just how these sand grains came to be cemented together makes a lively geological puzzle. Further, the exact cause of the colouring of some of the rocks is still little understood; even if there is plenty of reddish iron staining, the grey and green formations still give their problems. I noticed that highly attractive rock features occurred where quartzite had been enclosed between sandstone planes.

On an evening September walk at Langford Heathfield plenty of the unusual wild plant Sneezewort was found as well as the shrub Guelder-rose, with its many clusters of large, red and shiny berries. As darkness fell, moths were lured with the aid of a powerful mercury-vapour lamp. Fourteen moth species were identified, including the Large and the Lesser Yellow Underwing. The commonest moth to be attracted to the light was the Brimstone. Just why moths, or at least certain species of them, fly towards a light appears to remain a mystery; they do not fly towards the sun by day, nor in the direction of a full moon at night, yet an artificial light source is something they cannot resist, even if injury should happen as a result.

A search for fungi in September proved to be an enjoyable occasion, with pleasant walks along the rides of Cockercombe; however, fungi were not numerous and most were slug-eaten. This autumn, on the Quantock Hills, I think fungi have been below-average in quantity; for instance, I have had only one good feed of Field Mushrooms, although meals of Parasols and Field Blewits have been worthwhile and, perhaps, made up for the deficiency.

In late October, on a really cold day, I identified thirty-seven species of birds on a walk by the River Otter. One intriguing find was that of a small spherical nest built of woven, dried grasses in a hedge bush. This was a used nest of the minute Harvest Mouse, with a side entrance: I was delighted to see it. Then, near a pond, a song comprising a loud jumble of notes was heard from the base of a hedge, associated with a rapid mouse-like movement of a small bird which disappeared in the undergrowth. This can only have been a male Cetti's Warbler, which sings for much of the year and has extended its range in southern England in recent years. This was an exciting identification, only possible because of the bird's unexpected song; the abrupt notes were melodious even if the sequence was without a recognisable pattern. The Cetti's Warbler, a resident, is plump and red-brown; no doubt this bird was provoked into singing because it was disturbed by people walking nearby. At the time, the wind was too chilling to expect to see any autumn-flying dragonflies, but in October I was told a story by a lady about a large dragonfly which was in flight at Timsbury earlier in the month. This proved to be a female Southern Hawker which, sadly, had had its head bitten off by a cat near a garden pond where, I suspect, it had been attempting to egg-lay. Remarkably, the headless dragonfly remained for a week clinging to the side of a coal-bunker, until it died during an overnight frost. Presumably the insect could cling and adjust its position because of segmental reflex action. For this, no head is necessary.

On a larger scale, Red Deer stags moved into the Quantock moors and woods in October in moderately large numbers – in fact, more than have been seen in recent years. The autumn rut can be spectacular when several large stags are about; roaring to maintain the hind herds takes place by day as well as at night, but mainly at dawn and dusk. The bellowing vocalizations of Red Deer stags has a fascination and, late one evening, I recall toiling up a bracken slope towards the sounds to come face to face with a giant just over the brow of a hill. The massive, complex antlers were well-camouflaged against dead Bracken clumps and the large size of the stag relative to the several hinds present was evident; unfortunately, the animal turned and made off with his harem, across the moor and into the dimness of the evening. While stags utter their well-known roars of possession during the rut, on occasions a succession of urging, grunting sounds is produced. So far, I have been unable to guess at the meaning of these unusual but characteristic vocalizations. At times one comes across a stag which roars in a tenor rather than a bass tone; probably, tape-recordings could help in the identification of an individual stag. Unfortunately the rutting season is all too short and Red Deer stags are almost mute for the rest of the year.

Strangely, cool weather conditions did not stop two small bats flying as daylight faded over the southern Quantocks in late November. Indeed, a Mistle Thrush chased one of the bats as it fed, presumably, on flying insects which must have been rather scanty in numbers at the time. But the bat easily evaded the Mistle Thrush, which soon decided it was time to retire to roost in the shelter of the top of a Scots Pine. Still later in the year, in mid-December with the temperature little above freezing, I again saw a small bat in flight at dusk. It flew well and speedily but I felt that its quest for flying food could not have been well rewarded, if at all; maybe bats are getting hardier to venture out on a chill December evening. Then, at dawn in early December, again on the Quantocks, I was surprised to spot three Collared Doves arranged like vultures round the squashed carcass of a Rabbit on a road. Remarkably, the doves picked out and swallowed small portions of Rabbit flesh; of course, they could also have taken vegetable material from the ruptured intestinal tract of the dead animal. Usually we expect to see Magpies and Carrion Crows gorging on rabbit road casualties; somehow I doubt if I will ever again observe doves as meat-eaters. Still, it is always thrilling to watch the feeding behaviour of birds, especially when it appears to be so abnormal. Yet there is nothing unusual should a Mistle Thrush, dramatically, claim a laden Holly bush as its own feeding site. The powerful bird, Britain's largest song bird, will guard the bush and chase off intruders with harsh, grating churrs of annoyance. Hollies have been well-berried this autumn and, as well as Mistle Thrushes, Blackbirds, Fieldfares, Redwings, Starlings and Wood Pigeons have been feasting on this food source.

A Christmas Day walk; *birds in spring; strange amphibian and bird pairings; helping a hibernating Dormouse; a Grass-snake swallows a frog. Late 1993, early 1994*

The afternoon of Christmas Day is always a suitable time for a country walk and certainly there was plenty to look at in Quantock woods near my house at the end of 1993. At least three Dunnocks gave snatches of squeaky warblings and chased each other through Bramble clumps and, probably one or two silent females joined in as well; obviously, thoughts of territory-holding were in the minds of those birds that day. Actually the recommended English name for Dunnock is now the older one of Hedge Accentor; personally, I do not dislike the change. Happily for some, there has been no suggestion to alter the formal English name of Siskin and, on the same December afternoon, some fifty of these small, yellow, green and black finches were clinging, inverting and feeding at the tops of bare Beeches, Alders and Larches. It was a Christmas walk worth taking and, properly, was amidst melting snow. Like Siskins, Woodcocks are winter visitors to local woods but behaviour could hardly show greater differences. Instead of active and vocal small birds which readily feed in full view of people, the much larger, long-billed, plump, red-brown and mottled wader lies hidden in leaf-litter by day. Woodcocks feed at dusk or at night, probing their sensitive bills deep into mud by streams, so they can never be far from water; they were not uncommon on the Quantocks last winter.

Another bird which likes to be near water, is the Pied Wagtail and, during January, some twenty to thirty birds assembled at dusk to roost in a hedge at the village where I live. The calling wagtails, black-and-white and very conspicuous, mixed with chirping House Sparrows near stables before they finally settled to rest in bushes for the darkness of the cold winter night. In some areas, some hundreds of Pied Wagtails will meet up in winter to roost on glasshouses, in reed-beds or even on motorway service stations. In the last week of January I heard two male Chaffinches in full but brief song, so I knew that springtime was on its way on the Quantocks. At around the same time, the occasional wintering male Blackcap was glimpsed, living on what berries it could locate; such birds are certainly from the north and will migrate to Scandinavia or Germany in March or April. Another indication of the year's advance is the aerial display and varied croaking of Ravens over the hills – in February nest-building will commence. Occasionally, one comes across birds which are partly white but are not true albinos. I was reminded of this by a white-headed Hedge Accentor which was about in my garden in February and March, before it suddenly disappeared.

Moving from birds, Common Frogs and Common Toads were becoming noisy and active at some local ponds around this time – perhaps too active on some occasions. Thus, I saw two floating balls of writhing male Common Toads with a helpless female at the centre; in one case the female was smothered and drowned. Later, I saw a male Common Frog mount and grasp the floating, dead female toad; such is the sexual drive of the male amphibian in spring! Another unusual association I noticed this spring was between a male Pheasant and a solitary Guineafowl. This pair was together for several weeks near a plantation; well, it could be argued that the Guineafowl (presumably a female) was not true wildlife – but it was certainly a free-living bird, in the same sense as the introduced Pheasant. I do not know the outcome of this particular liaison.

In April a walk in a gale along the coast at Kilve showed a grouping of small, dark finches over ploughland; pale rumps confirmed that this was a flock of Twites on migration. As this was April, I was not surprised to see a fresh, lichened ovoid nest of a Long-tailed Tit pair; the nest, however, was in a tangle of Madder, which is a new site for this species for me. Later in April along the Kilve coast lots of interesting spring flowers were found and a hunting Peregrine conveniently allowed excellent views.

Of course, birds are not the only creatures to have nests in April. For example, I came across a small ball of a nest in a fern stock and covered by dead willow leaves, at least, partly so. The nest was composed of the rind or bast of Honeysuckle and had been partly opened (maybe by a Fox) and there was a honey-coloured, already stirring adult Dormouse but still in its hibernaculum.[14] The brown, bushy tail lay obliquely across the abdomen, with the tip at the face of the flexed, curled-up animal. Before leaving, I put a covering of more dead, dry willow leaves over the Dormouse; even so, it was a warm day and I think it was quite ready to face the problems of outdoor life. On the Quantock Hills many people remarked that they heard fewer Cuckoos than usual in song during May. My impression is that fewer Cuckoos were around than in 1993 and I did not discover any Cuckoo eggs; perhaps Cuckoos had fared badly on their spring migration. It was reported nationally that Willow Warblers (Britain's commonest migrant) were scarce this spring; however, as breeding birds I thought that numbers on the Quantocks were at the usual level. Wood Warblers too nested in their usual haunts; at one nest I observed there were definitely three individuals feeding the young in June. I suppose an adult Wood Warbler had joined in after failing to attract a mate itself.

In summer, one cannot watch wildlife without being aware of predation. Hence, on the Mendips, I watched a Hobby as it seized and

14 A Dormouse about to wake from winter slumbers in its hibernating nest on the ground. Summer breeding nests are often surprisingly high up in bushes, and may be spotted on a Quantocks walk after leaves have fallen in autumn.

ate large dragonflies as it flew with amazing agility, even discarding the unwanted insect wings. Then, quite unexpectedly, I saw a medium-sized Grass-snake beginning to swallow a docile female Common Frog, head-first; of course, I was quite unprepared to photograph this event! Around the same time, I watched a Sparrowhawk circling and gliding high in the air when, suddenly, it swooped at remarkable speed behind some trees. When I walked to that place next day, there was a liberal scattering of Woodpigeon feathers: clearly, the pigeon had been killed, and probably carried off, by a female Sparrowhawk. A female Sparrowhawk can carry a Woodpigeon in its talons, but the load is too heavy for the smaller male. As the summer progressed I have seen increasing numbers of butterflies, which were relatively scarce earlier. Dragonflies, in general, have not been in large numbers but I have been pleased to see two species at locations where I have not noted them in previous years. If I can photograph a dragonfly satisfactorily, then I can be sure of the identification and, on this basis, I have found that both Black-tailed Skimmers and Ruddy Darters have been in good numbers, relatively speaking, this summer and, probably have extended their ranges. I feel there is always pleasure in spotting newly emerged dragonflies and thinking of them as they will be after attaining full, adult colouring.**[15]**

Similarly, when I discovered a newly-born Red Deer calf in a birch copse in early June,**[16]** I recalled that the Red Deer rut and belling would be due in October. October is a good month for the hooting of Tawny Owls, often occasioned by the young of the year trying to mark out territorial boundaries. When watching a pensive, newly-flown juvenile Tawny Owl on a forest branch in late May, I thought of the same bird calling in competition at dusk in the autumn to come – when it would no longer be supplied with food by its parents.**[17]** To survive, aggression is needed in the wild.

15 Black-tailed Skimmers, at least the males as this one, have a habit of sunning themselves on open ground in their territories. They are very vigilant and difficult to approach closely.

16 A Red Deer calf in June, lying amongst Whortleberry vegetation in a Quantocks valley, and just waiting for a milk drink from its mother. Calves are usually well concealed in herbage; they lie very still but become active when the mother visits. Calves are suckled for several months, even after they are fully mobile, and stay with the hind for about a year.

17 This young Tawny Owl, photographed in May, had recently flown from its tree nesting cavity on Aisholt Common; it awaits the night when, hopefully, a parent will bring in a mouse or vole breakfast. Young Tawny Owls depend on their parents for food for several weeks after leaving the nest.

The Magpie Fungus and Slippery Jack; a Rough-legged Buzzard; Red Deer ticks and birds; Bullfinches and their long-lived nests. Later 1994

When walking in mixed mature woodland near Aisholt early in October looking for fungi, the species which most impressed me was the Magpie Fungus. I do not find the Magpie often and, really, it is rather spectacular with a brown conical cap, flecked with white patches. Happily, several Magpie specimens were seen in a particular part of the wood and some over-mature ones were dripping a black ink from the liquifying gills. No, I was not tempted to gather any Magpies to eat but I did pick good numbers of Field Mushrooms on pasture land on the Quantocks in September; these made excellent eating and excess pickings were placed in the deep-freeze. Near Scots Pines on Exmoor I came across a vigorous growth of slimy, brown-capped pored fungi in late September. These large boletus-type agarics had a distinct flavour when cooked and made a really palatable meal. This was 'Slippery Jack' which some people do not choose to eat because it is so slimy, but a knowing few will search for it when they want a special treat. Now, who's for eating 'Slippery Jack'?

In early December, there were still good edible fungi available on the Quantocks. Rings of Field Blewits, not always complete, grew well amongst long grass in two or three fields. The stalk is short, thick and amethyst coloured, while the cap is a pale grey-brown; this stocky fungus is well-flavoured and best, in my view, when cooked with bacon. While it has been a good year for edible fungi, it has also been favourable for poisonous ones. I have seen more Death-caps than usual – mostly slug-eaten, as is commonplace. Those I have found have all been associated with oaks; somehow, there is an air of foreboding about these yellow-green caps with their tissue-paper rings and remnants but, unfortunately, not everyone gets such a feeling. I understand that, again this year, several persons have died from Death-cap poisoning in Europe, mostly from the central region. In addition, Liberty Caps, producing dangerous hallucinations if eaten, were common on some Quantock grasslands, well into December.

Unlike fungi, certain birds move around a lot in autumn and, in September, several groups of Redwings from the north were feeding on Hawthorn berries locally. Then, in mid-October, high over the Quantock slopes, a large Buzzard was spotted in the distance and, as it approached me, it went into a speedy glide and disappeared to the south. When overhead, I saw that the bird had a pale tail with a black transverse terminal band. Clearly this was a Rough-legged Buzzard, and a winter visitor from the arctic tundra. I believe that several Rough-legged

Buzzards have been sighted in eastern England this autumn but this is the only one I have come across in the west. I am not familiar with the species but, in flight and as a glider, it is certainly an expert.

In late October I took a walk along the banks of the River Otter. I was intrigued to watch a big immature Herring Gull repeatedly plunge-dive into deep, swirling estuary water and surface with some dark-coloured food material which was eagerly swallowed; strangely none of the many other gulls present nearby joined in the food hunt. Obviously, the nature of the meal must remain a mystery. As expected, one of the commonest birds of the estuary was the raucous, introduced Canada Goose and, amongst a large flock, two small Barnacle Geese, with their white cheeks, were noted. One questioned if the Barnacle Geese, which had probably summered in arctic zones, now considered themselves part of the Canada Goose population. Another interesting item of behaviour was when two Carrion Crows repeatedly hovered, in clumsy fashion, low over a particular area of salt-marsh. I assumed that the crows were hovering in anticipation, waiting to pounce on some tasty live prey, but no pouncing occurred; moreover, no small bird, mammal or reptile could be detected through binoculars, and which might have attracted the crows. I find it pleasing, at times, for a bird's behaviour to remain a puzzle.

However, when Magpies, Starlings or Jackdaws perch on the backs of Red Deer on the Quantock Hills, their behaviour can readily be explained. The remarkable Red Deer rut occurred during October and, at dawn, when rutting behaviour was most intense, it was not uncommon to see a Magpie on a deer's back as light became adequate. The Magpies search for and eat ticks or other invertebrates on the coats of the deer and, sometimes, they are given a really rough journey. I recall one Magpie which was perched on a big dominant stag as it roared, raced round to deter intruders and mounted its favoured hinds; amazingly, the Magpie clung on to the pelt of the animal, seemingly enjoying its ride and quite forgetting to search for food.

On another occasion, by a Somerset reservoir in early December, I watched a horde of Black-headed Gulls, screaming and swooping, dashing at innocent Tufted Ducks as they surfaced after diving. Any food which the ducks had not swallowed was at once pirated, just as skuas will steal fish from hard-working terns while in flight. On the same reservoir I saw some ten Goosanders swimming; these powerful saw-billed ducks, both male and female, were diving too but the Black-Headed Gulls ignored them. Presumably the gulls knew that Goosanders do not give up hard-won food readily.

For certain land birds, some food is obtained by hard work and in small packets. Thus, during the autumn, I watched a party of Bullfinches feeding on Blackberry remnants. A seed was pulled from one drupe at a time and then, only after cutting through the seed-coat with the bill was the food available; a lot of industry is necessary to get much of a meal from this source as the fruit pulp does not interest Bullfinches and is discarded. Of course, Bullfinches can be highly voracious when they eat cultivated fruit and flower buds. This annoying behaviour takes place in late winter or early spring when seeds such as Blackberry, Rowan or Elder have all been consumed; in compensation, one has a sight of the Bullfinches, including the handsome rose-red breast of the males. Not long back I picked up a male Bullfinch which had concussed itself by flying into a glass panel, perhaps escaping from a Sparrowhawk; apart from admiring the colouring, I was surprised by the soft and silky texture of the plumage. On recovery, the Bullfinch flew off displaying its white rump – one of nature's white signals which enable the birds to keep together in their natural habitat of dimly lit woodland. It is said that Bullfinches pair for life; often cock and hen are seen together in winter but unless they have been ringed or tagged I cannot see that pairing can be proved. I am always delighted if I hear the musical, piping calls of Bullfinches, even if I have failed to spot the shy, retiring bird itself. In spring, the male Bullfinch does not sing loudly from a tree in the manner of a Song Thrush or a Chaffinch; the song is merely a creaky jumble of call-notes, which must serve to attract and keep a mate – also, it must be remembered that the hen sings as well. Perhaps understandably, from the type of woodland habitat, another shy bird, the Hawfinch, sings in a similar way.

The Bullfinch's nest is distinctive and easily recognised: a neat cup of hairs and rootlets is built on a strong base of interwoven twiglets. This twiglet foundation may persist for years, after the cup has been blown away; as an example, I always inspect one in a particular Quantock Hawthorn as I pass, although I suppose it will disintegrate one day. Is it coincidence that both the Jay and the Hawfinch have evolved nests of the same pattern? Young Bullfinches can be told from adults as they lack black caps; perhaps curiously for finches, they remain quite unstreaked. As is well known, a feature of a juvenile Goldfinch, Siskin or Greenfinch is its streaked body plumage.

It proved to be a mild autumn and early winter and dragonflies were on the wing relatively late in the year – I think Common Darters, Southern Hawkers or Migrant Hawkers. I believe that dragonfly sightings, in general, went on to early November in 1994 in southern England. Quite a few late-flying butterflies were seen too and I observed many Speckled Woods. Excitingly for me, I saw Clouded Yellow butterflies in August and in September in Somerset; I assume these had emerged locally. I watched one Clouded Yellow in flight as I peered directly at a Kingfisher on a willow branch near the Doniford stream: I feel it is always a triumph to be able to combine notable natural history observations, as on that occasion. I do not know how Kingfishers fared in breeding last year but a few birds certainly nested late in the season: I saw Goldfinches feeding young in the nest in August, while a newly-flown Song Thrush was food-begging nearby.

Of course, both Song Thrushes and Goldfinches may have second or third broods in July, if the food supply is adequate.[18] I write now in December as the cries of Red Foxes begin to be heard in woodland at night and the pungent scent markings of the males add interest to any Quantocks walk. Coupled with this, the occasional expertly camouflaged Woodcock will rise unexpectedly at one's feet from oak or beech leaf litter, to fly off noisily to another resting place. Woodcocks fly off near dusk to feed in the mud near streams; in the trees, Tawny Owls hoot on waking and Robins tick loudly before they fly to the shelter of their roosting cover.

18 Two-day-old Song Thrush nestlings, apparently thriving, on their nest-lining of dried mud and decayed wood, which was moulded and shaped by their mother's breast. Their father, having now to find food for his chicks, will not have much time for singing and serenading his mate.

The Rough-legged Buzzard again; a Willow Warbler's protective behaviour; a Hobby catches dragonflies. Earlier 1995

There was no shortage of rain as the year started. Where I live on the Quantock Hills I had a rainfall average of 5.52mm for January and 4.23mm for February. However, some birds appear to enjoy singing in the rain and, temperatures being reasonable in January, there was good song heard from Mistle and Song Thrush, Wren and also Robin. Clearly certain birds have territories in mind, as did a local Great Spotted Woodpecker which drummed with vigour on several leafless trees. Did it get a headache in consequence? I was pleased to be invited to look at a possible Rough-legged Buzzard on the northern aspect of the Quantocks one day in early February and spent some hours searching through binoculars, although without suspicion of success. But, on driving away, I saw a Buzzard-like bird perched high on a Scots Pine; on stopping the car conveniently nearby, I noted a large, upright raptor with a pale head and a very dark lower breast: clearly, this was the individual I was seeking.

The Rough-legged Buzzard was probably in its first winter and a visitor from Scandinavia; no doubt it left England in early spring. But it is likely that the next scarce bird species I saw was at least a British resident. Not

19 A male Beautiful Demoiselle, the largest of the British damselflies; these striking insects fly in summer over Somerset's fast-flowing hill streams. Males will flutter in display flights to attract females, with colour shades varying according to the incidence of sunlight. Females are duller, with metallic green shades which, again, vary with the light; Beautiful Demoiselles are magical insects to encounter while walking by Quantock and Exmoor streams.

far from Bishop's Lydeard I watched a small blue-grey falcon with very pointed wings flying and twisting low over a ploughed field; the size was about that of a Mistle Thrush – doubtless the bird was a male Merlin, perhaps on its way back to moorland breeding-grounds. One had the impression that it could surprise and out-fly almost any unwary small bird which was feeding or resting; I expect that in its nesting territory Meadow Pipits are the common victims. Then, a few days later I observed a much larger falcon soaring over a combe before it entered into a steep glide: on this occasion a roaming Peregrine failed to close on a lone Woodpigeon.

In late March I saw a solitary Swallow in flight near a farm, although I did not sight another until mid-April. In late March, Small Tortoiseshell, Peacock and Brimstone butterflies were about when it was sunny, just as the Chiffchaffs arrived and the cocks started to sing. By this time, a Quantock Raven's nest held four hungry young, which were still being brooded by their mother during cold spells. The young Ravens left their nest at the end of April; evidently they had good appetites and called with harsh, demanding and rasping cries when an adult approached. Yet I heard other calls while they were still in the nest; soon after dawn certain pleasing, murmuring and almost musical sounds were uttered, as though the nestlings were greeting a new day or perhaps each other.

It is said that Willow Warblers are scarce in Britain this year, perhaps due to faring badly during migration in Africa. Nevertheless, the Quantocks certainly have a reasonable breeding population this summer and, by late June, several young birds were on the wing. One nest I had under observation lost its nestlings, sadly, at three days, with the young probably taken by a Jay or Magpie; strangely I found that the nest's lining of feathers had quite disappeared too. Evidently some bird had carried off the feathers as welcome prizes to line its own nest. At another Willow Warbler's nest, situated under flattened dead bracken, I happened to walk by as the mature young were flying out strongly to nearby bush cover, leaving, as I thought, an empty nest. I was surprised; therefore, to see a parent fly to hover and call over the vacated one; on checking, I found that no nestling remained and no ground predator was lurking in the herbage. I was further surprised when I returned that way about an hour later to see an adult Willow Warbler again hovering and calling over the site of the empty nest. If the Willow Warbler's puzzling behaviour was caused by the previous presence of an unseen enemy by the nest, then the reaction to it was remarkably sustained.

Dragonflies seem to be in average numbers at their usual haunts. I saw my first Beautiful Demoiselle for the year by the River Yarty and, later in the month, single individuals were noted by the Quantock streams.[19] On a June visit to the Mendip Hills, I was delighted to spot a fine Downy Emerald dragonfly. Now a scarce species; this was a male which glinted in the sun, showing the dark bronze colouring of its abdomen. Also in June, the large Emperor dragonflies appeared to be well distributed, although I saw many more males than females; certainly the enamelled blue abdomen with its black streak down the back is an attractive feature of this tireless flier. Another apparently tireless flier I watched over the Mendips was an agile female Hobby, which was chasing dragonflies. The small falcon chased and swooped with remarkable ease, seizing larger dragonflies in a talon; it often ate the insects in the air or else descended to a dead willow to enjoy its meal, after tearing off the wings.

One expects to see young birds in the woods in late June and often the calls of the parents give clues as to their whereabouts. One morning I was alerted that a Redstart family was about by the anxiety calls of the male parents and, not far distant, fledgling Chiffchaffs stayed in beechen cover as an adult gave alarm cries. Moving on to the Quantock heather moorland, the tapping and high-frequency notes of both male and female Stonechat suggested that young were out of the nest; satisfactorily, I soon saw three free-flying juveniles scattered in hawthorns. Surely, the quality of any patch of heath or moor is enhanced if Stonechats or Whinchats keep it as breeding territory. Perhaps it is equally pleasing if, as I experienced recently in Somerset, one sees a male and a female Siskin feeding near conifers in June; is that not very suggestive, although not proof, of attempted breeding? Siskins now regularly take peanuts in many Somerset gardens in winter; it would be most gratifying to know that these dainty and colourful small finches are beginning to nest commonly near our villages.

Fungi and rain; dawn fungus picking; birds' nesting patterns; a Spotted Flycatcher's butterfly meal. Later 1995

Because we had a hot July and August, I anticipated that we would have a good fungal season, and so it proved. When fungal mycelium is well baked then, when rains come, fruiting bodies sprout up at remarkable speed. There is nothing more pleasing then gathering Field Mushrooms in September in damp pastures as Swallows swoop low and round one's legs, cropping the evening flies. Higher up in the air, House Martins chase their flies, taking their food in small portions, while the mushroom picker looks forward to a planned supper of unique flavour. By October the large Horse Mushrooms were appearing – often twice the size of Field Mushrooms and really fleshy, succulent and delicious. I found that if I went out before dawn to listen to Red Deer stags belling on the Quantock Hills, I could return as light appeared and, with luck, gather a few Horse Mushrooms from their rings in grassy places; as I picked, so Carrion Crows, Ravens and Buzzards called as they flew from their overnight roosts. But mushrooms were not the only crop which it was worth searching for last autumn. Summer heat helped Sweet Chestnuts to mature and ripen, and the flavour was excellent. Understandably, there was competition for these tasty nuts from Grey Squirrels and Red Deer.

In mid-October at Cockercombe no fewer than fifty-five fungal species were identified and amongst these, four were worthy of special mention. These can only be referred to by their scientific names as no popular ones exist; as such, they have mycological interest but, hopefully, the names will stimulate any enquiring naturalist to seek more information about them. One specimen was *Boletus pulverolentus*, a small pored agaric whose yellow flesh turns a dark blue very quickly if cut or injured; a second pored fungus was *Porphyrellus pseudoscaber*, a rare brown agaric usually associated with conifers, and a new record for the area. Then an unusual parasol-type fungus discovered was *Lepiota castallea*, with a small, scaly red-brown cap; further, a specimen of *Amanita gemmata* was spotted under a spruce. *A. gemmata* has a pallid yellow cap with a stem ring and a basal volva; it looks rather like a false death cap but is said to be very poisonous. Yet, one author I read stated that the taste was 'pleasant'; personally, I do not think I will try and confirm this statement!

Yes, it has been a colourful fungal autumn, with some species fruiting until late in the year. I found hallucinatory Liberty Caps, with their pointed tops, in fields in early December and so it was with certain dung black-spored fungi. Indeed, in late December I came across a ragged Stinkhorn, this was the latest date I can recall seeing one and, unsurprisingly, I found no evidence of any attracted flies. Once, in autumn, I saw a Robin investigating flies on a Stinkhorn phallus – but with a very different ambient temperature. But Robins were about in that piece of woodland in mid-winter and both male and female sang at dawn and towards dusk. It is strange, I feel, that hen Robins, as chats, defend winter territories; interestingly, some recent research has demonstrated that the concentration of male sex hormone rises in female Robins in winter. With most European birds, naturally, the amount of male sex hormone in the blood (with males) is maximal during March and April – as one would have expected. I doubt whether hormone estimations have been carried out on female birds in winter apart from Robins, as there is normally no song from the others and no claiming of winter territory.

Another piece of academic research which intrigued me concerned Stonechats. It appears that male Stonechats which sing a lot are better at guarding their nests, and feeding their young, than those cocks with little inclination to sing. As far as I know, this association has not been proved with other species of small birds, certainly not those which breed on moorland. Actually, song is not usually an obvious feature with male Stonechats but when it occurs it is a rather brief, twittering warble. With the Whinchat (the moorland bird with the white stripe above the eye) the cock's song is a far more persistent warble, often enlivened by mimicry – for example, worthy imitations of the calls of the Curlew. Superficially, Whinchats and Stonechats look somewhat similar, especially the females, and their anxiety calls are much alike; both species nest on the Quantocks, with the Stonechat being a resident and the Whinchat a summer migrant. To keep their numbers, Stonechats have two and often three broods while Whinchats, with the added hazard of migration to and from Africa, maintain their population with just one nest although, just occasionally, two broods are reared. Stonechats build their first nest at the end of March or in early April but Whinchats do not arrive until April or May; the ground nests of both species are very well hidden, but that of the Stonechat is the most difficult to locate. It is always gratifying, I think, to come upon a carried half egg shell of Whinchat or Stonechat on a Somerset moor, so indicating that hatching, at least, has been successful with these colourful, patterned and sometimes demonstrative birds.

One attractive Somerset bird is the Goldfinch, and in a nest I had under observation, the young hatched in the first week of July. Feeding was infrequent and I never saw an adult approach the nest with a caterpillar in its bill, as would have happened with a Chaffinch. The answer is that Goldfinches feed their young by regurgitation of a food mass – probably already partly digested. As with most Goldfinch nests, this one was well concealed by a leafy spray but, even so, I noted that its walls became increasingly whitened by droppings. The parents remove the nestlings' faecal sacs up to five days but then the nest becomes increasingly conspicuous; however, this is often not obvious because of effective leaf cover. By mid July the young had flown, to scatter in nearby trees – each calling musically to stress the need for food to a vigilant parent. On the same day, I watched a parent Spotted Flycatcher feed a Peacock butterfly entire to a free-flying juvenile: the butterfly was swallowed with ease. Yet when a male Spotted Flycatcher, in courtship, feeds its mate, a Peacock butterfly will have its wings pulled off beforehand; probably the gape of the adult is less able to stretch than that of a young bird.[20]

Peacock butterflies bred well in the Quantock area last summer; also, I saw one Holly Blue – this species was almost completely absent in 1994. Perhaps seeking water, a Silver-washed Fritillary flew into my cottage in early August; happily, numbers of this spectacular butterfly were reasonable in nearby woodland. Then Dark Green Fritillaries were seen near the River Barle when looking for ferns in August, but there was no

20 A Spotted Flycatcher with prey for its young, probably a hover-fly. It is sad that Spotted Flycatchers have so declined in numbers in Britain recently; they used to be common breeding birds in Somerset gardens and churchyards. I expect there have been problems in their African wintering zones or along the migration routes; certainly the liberal use of insecticide chemicals has meant extra danger.

sight or even a suspicion of a High Brown Fritillary. In the same month, I found a Purple Hairstreak butterfly drowned in a water bucket in my garden: a sad end to a beautiful insect. The dryness and heat of late summer seemed to favour Small Coppers over the Quantocks and so it was with Commas, Small Tortoiseshells, Painted Ladies and, in particular, Red Admirals.[21]

Most dragonfly species liked the heat too, although pond levels dropped alarmingly in August. One dragonfly species I spotted in late summer on Mendip was the Yellow-winged Darter; it seems that large numbers of these insects flew over the English Channel from mainland Europe last summer and infiltrated across England. It was an exciting find and it was satisfying to photograph it too. Ruddy Darters, once so rare, were in good numbers; remarkably, I saw one female, held in tandem, laying her eggs on dry earth and some distance from water or even mud. It is sad to think of fertile Ruddy Darter eggs being wasted! I was interested to see some Ruddy Darter males being chased by the newly-arrived Yellow-winged Darters and which also flew after Black Darters; presumably even these invading dragonflies sensed that their newly-won territories were under threat.

21 Green-veined white butterflies mating. They are named from the underside wing markings; food plants include Cuckoo Flower and Jack-by-the-Hedge. I am always amazed by the often quite unexpected positions seen when butterflies pair!

Aided by the high summer temperatures, wasps were common in Somerset and so were Hornets in wooded places. I had one Hornet nest under observation, and activity did not cease until the first week in November. Hornets are worth watching; they catch and bring in flies or even bees to feed to their larvae and once, surprisingly, I saw a spider carried into the nest. The sounds are fascinating too; often a fanner will work away regulating nest temperature but only to be interrupted as an adult flies in with food. Vibratory noise occurs as a Hornet wingbeats in a confined space and the nest's paper cells are commonly being added to or modified. I was surprised too by the amount of night activity which went on; on hot nights the Hornets arrived and departed as Tawny Owls hooted from neighbouring trees. Birds appeared to disregard the Hornets, although on one occasion I saw a Blue Tit attack a resting insect which flew off speedily.

I write now in the chill of winter and it is difficult to think of a large Emperor dragonfly being trapped and killed on a spider's web, but it was only last July when I came across evidence of this. Where spiders build webs with firm anchorage, as on gorse, it seems that damsel and dragonflies are common victims, but I cannot think that the powerful Emperor dragonflies get trapped very often. More likely, they will be chased and seized by Hobbies, those speedy small falcons which specialise in dragonflies as prey. At present, in cold December rain, migratory Redwings eat up our crop of Holly berries and noisy Mistle Thrush parties roam the hills in search of food. Small Goldfinch flocks scatter and twitter as they seek weed seeds; this reminds me that last August I saw a Goldfinch trapped inside a garden fruit cage. As I went to release the finch, I noticed that it was followed outside the cage by a Chiffchaff – as though it wished to be sociable! More recently, a few days ago I was delighted to see a flock of some fifty wading birds flying south near the Mendip Hills. Wings were pointed and dark at the tips; at its base, the wing was very white. Clearly these were Golden rather than Grey Plovers; I wondered where these birds had been hatched. While it is pleasing to watch birds in winter, I think there is greater pleasure in spring. It is not long now to February when Cuckoos in Africa will fly north across the Sahara; hopefully, several of them will end their migratory journey in Somerset next April.

Blue Anchor Bay; autumn on the River Otter; Pied Wagtails in Taunton; Dragonflies and deer; Hawk-moth caterpillars; strange behaviour of the Fly-Catchers. Later 1996

In late summer I took a few walks to the east along the beach at Blue Anchor Bay – after having ensured that the tide was well out! Certainly it is a good place to spot a dashing Peregrine; these speedy falcons seem to favour that coast although the cliffs do not have the height or grandeur of those in North Cornwall where I have previously watched the birds. Considering the Peregrine's ability to launch into accelerated flight, any pigeon, whatever the species, would be well advised to avoid that coast or even crossing the Bristol Channel. The occasional heap of pigeon feathers tells its sombre story.

One attraction of Blue Anchor Bay is an exposure of alabaster, pink and soft and contrasting pleasantly in colour with the grey layers of mudstone.[22] I understand that this attractive stone is anhydrite which, chemically, is mainly calcium sulphate; this has been deposited because of precipitation following evaporation from sea-water, perhaps in a lagoon. Gypsum is also calcium sulphate, with added water, and is used in preparing plasters and cement. The Blue Anchor alabaster is a delicate pink in colour, so something must be added as calcium sulphate is white. Iron salts have been suggested but are there other impurities? Blue Anchor alabaster fades to whiteness if exposed to sunlight for several months, or at least that happens in my garden – would that occur if iron compounds had caused the coloration? I once saw a fellow naturalist pick up a piece of alabaster, quite convinced that it was a pink quartz which, of course, is a hard silica rock; however, a light scraping with a knife soon convinced him that the resulting powder was more likely to be that of calcium sulphate! Blue Anchor Bay has fine and varied geological features and is an ideal place for a stimulating winter walk – but do choose a time when the tide is retreating!

In late summer Shelducks moult in Bridgwater Bay and, when the ducks eventually become more mobile, the Blue Anchor coast is attractive to them. At a distance, the large, almost goose-like bird looks black-and-white but really it is beautifully coloured when fully feathered, especially when there is a good view of its chestnut body band and red bill. By November, Shelducks have mainly acquired their full colouring after the moult and can be seen as the tide recedes, searching for small crabs or marine worms in shallow water, or resting or swimming in groups on the sea just a few yards out from the shore. Parties of another red-billed bird are common along the same shore too, although the beaks are long and probing and of the wader type: the handsome

22 An exposed area of alabaster in a seam at Blue Anchor. Alabaster is evaporated from water which contained calcium sulphate or gypsum; the rock is pink due to impurities. There is a big alabaster seam at Blue Anchor which extends as far as Watchet.

Oystercatcher. Oystercatcher parties are noisy with their piping high-pitched cries and, judging by the large number of sand worm-casts revealed by the out-going tide, there is no shortage of worm food for those Oystercatchers which do not want to attack the local mussels.

At the River Otter estuary in October, a single Kingfisher was watched perched on successive branches at the river bank, and which dived repeatedly and briefly for fishy food in the shallow, flowing water. It was impressive how the colour shade of the blue-green, sheeny upper parts of the bird altered, depending on the reflected sunlight of varying intensity. Yes, the birds which drew my attention were colourful, but there was real interest about others of duller plumage and this included Meadow and Rock Pipits; was I really sure that I was not looking at Tawny, Water or Tree Pipits? Perhaps more acrobatic in behaviour than the Rock Pipits were several Pied Wagtails, of varying ages and of both sexes, which gave a spirited demonstration of aerial flycatching from a muddy slope – rising to snap up flies which were profuse over Glasswort and Seablite patches.

A few dragonflies appeared as the day progressed and the air was warmed. At least three male Migrant Hawkers were on the wing, with blue spots on a brown, segmented body; this species, however, is known as a late summer or autumn flier. Also recognised as an autumn flier is the Brown Hawker; three of these big, brown-winged dragonflies were in flight and others were spotted at rest on tree foliage. I had not expected to come across this dragonfly at that location and, foolishly, it rook me a long while to be sure of the identification. In August 1995 immigrant Yellow-winged Darters appeared in southern England and some probably mated. I wondered if I would see any of the same species this summer, bur I did not detect any of these colourful insects. Even so, the aquatic larvae probably spend two years in water, so maybe some will emerge next August.

I saw Oystercatchers and Shelduck on the walk. Indeed, there were plenty of birds to look at, of which perhaps the most numerous were Wigeons; one wondered from what northern lake area most of those had been hatched. Wigeons are vocal birds and the cheerful, distinctive whistles of the males contrasted with the hard, growling notes of the rather dull-looking females. Still, the bright yellow crown streak of the drake, along its chestnut head, makes up for the lack of conspicuous colouring for the female. There were lots of Teal, around a hundred, both resting and swimming; this is Europe's smallest duck, of which the male is attractively patterned with a green stripe across the eye and a chestnut head; in addition, there is a gold-yellow patch near the tail. Both sexes show the fine green wing patch or speculum.

Happily Pied Wagtails are common in Somerset and sometimes large numbers roost on town buildings. For instance, in early November, large numbers flitted round a Taunton car-park in the dusk. Eventually, most of the birds flew over the River Tone to settle on the roof of a warehouse: at least a hundred were involved.

I was glad to see that both Common and Black Darter dragonflies were in good numbers on the Mendip Hills and at some Quantock sites in late summer; perhaps surprisingly, Emperor dragonflies were plentiful too although I have always regarded them as mid-summer fliers. I saw my last autumn dragonfly for 1996 in late October and that was a male Migrant Hawker which was flying near West Bagborough. A few days earlier on a fine and sunny day, many dragonflies were on the wing at the Westhay Reserve on the Levels. I noted at least ten Common Darters sunning and two pairs were watched mating;[23] Migrant Hawkers seemed unusually numerous.

Turning to somewhat larger animals, October is a significant month on the Quantocks because of the gathering up and rutting of Red Deer. I got some good sightings of these powerful mammals, although often one hears rather than sees them. One must accept that, as daylight increases, so the deer retreat into woodland cover. This year, dawn

23 Common Darters mating, in the ring or wheel position, in August. These dragonflies are sometimes abundant in Somerset and may be seen in flight, or even egg-laying, in October. Garden ponds often attract this species and I have seen the female laying her eggs into the salty water of a river estuary (I have doubts as to whether any larvae hatched out!).

roaring was scanty but appeared to increase as gusting winds or storms arose; was this related, in fact, just to day length or were the storms really stimulatory?

One fungal species I always find eye-catching is the Red Boletus. I discovered two or three on the Quantocks in August; this agaric is large and fleshy with a red-brown cap, red pores and a bulky red stalk. The way the flesh quickly turns blue when it is injured is truly a magnificent chemical conjuring trick! I would not be tempted to eat a Red Boletus (although many boletus species have a wonderful flavour) but I do enjoy the Parasol mushroom, which grew well locally last autumn; the top of the cap has an artistic design of radiating brown scales. The flesh of the Parasol is sweet with quite a different flavour from that of the trusted and admirable Field Mushroom. There is also a Woodland Parasol which is smaller and is more shaggy in appearance – but is still good eating for most (but not all) people.

Fungi add interest to any autumnal woodland walk and this is often so even in December. Dead wood commonly bears purple, jelly-like convolutions which are Ascomycetes or spore-shooters, which one can observe, with luck, as visiting Woodcocks fly by for a twilight worm feed;

or, damp pastures can support Field Blewits, with their blue stalks which can constitute a really succulent country supper. Blewits, like all agarics or mushrooms are spore-droppers or Basidiomycetes: truly, all fungi are fascinating structures, whether the details can be seen with the naked eye or only through the microscope.

Following an amazing influx of Painted Lady butterflies, as immigrants, last June, they remained to breed on thistles and were still numerous in August. I wonder if the species will be commonplace next summer? Somehow I have my doubts. The caterpillars of Painted Ladies are not spectacular but those of hawk-moths are certainly eye-catching; Elephant Hawk-moth larvae seemed frequent last September, feeding on willow-herb or Fuchsia. These big, fleshy dark brown caterpillars are worth watching as they display their eye-spots or show the terminal horn. Another insect, which has been relatively common this autumn, has been the Red Wasp. I found that if I saw wasps entering a ground nest and if they were small, they were usually red ones, with a red line or two across the front of the yellow abdomen. Although small, Red Wasps have a vicious sting; when I am a victim I recall that only the females sting!

As is well known, Sheep-ticks are common on the Quantock Hills and on Exmoor and I found a few attached to me last summer – to be removed with great care. However, last August I came across a dead Great Tit with a fully engorged, large tick clinging to the front of its neck. What tick species was this? Foolishly, I failed to find the answer. August was notable for sightings of Hobbies, wheeling or swooping or being mobbed by Swallows in various parts of Somerset. On the Quantocks, I was surprised to see a Hobby on the ground in a moorland valley and which was, I believe, devouring some insect prey. I thought that was a strange situation for an agile Hobby but, anyway, it flew off at great speed after detecting my presence. Then, at dusk on an August evening, I saw a Spotted Flycatcher hawking for flies from the top of a conifer; reaching for my binoculars, I was most surprised to find that I was looking at ten or twelve of the birds fly-catching communally. This behaviour continued until it was too dark to see what was happening; were the birds locally-bred families which had joined up for an evening feed together or was this a true migratory party? I have never seen Spotted Flycatchers migrating together but I understand that does occur over the Mediterranean at times, probably by birds from eastern Europe. Nothing is certain about bird behaviour. Now for a final bird incident: in November, I watched a small party of Greenfinches opening rose hips to extract and eat the seeds; this is normal behaviour but, how do the finches avoid getting at least some of the barbed hooks stuck in the throat or on the tongue?

The spread of Collared Doves, Crows and Owls; Sparrowhawk attack over the shops of Taunton; picking mushrooms and surprising an Adder; birds' songs and nests. Earlier 1997

It was cold and icy in early January, but I was impressed by the frequent calling of Collared Doves in the Quantock villages. This repetitive yet musical calling is really a song, given by the male to advertise its presence and to attract and bond a mate; there is a separate flight call which is loud and rather nasal in quality and is produced by either sex. Many people find the cooing song of the Wood Pigeon equally monotonous, but it does have its champions who claim that it is preferable to the dove musically. Wood Pigeons, unlike Collared Doves, commonly frequent woodland, both deciduous and coniferous, but are also heard in parks and large gardens. I confess that I rather like the Collared Dove, with its pale buff appearance and black half collar; I am amazed that this relatively tame and common farm and village dove has spread north-west across Europe from Asia during the present century. Nests can be found in almost any month of the year, so singing males in January are commonplace. As Collared Doves originated from Asia, it is surprising that they seem to thrive in the chill of the British winter as well as in summer.

There is no surprise, however, if one sees Carrion Crows thriving in winter. Mostly, they look very well nourished, no doubt because of the ease of obtaining squashed rabbit carcasses from the roads and the presence of birds such as Redwings which have been made feeble by the cold and poor feeding. Carrion Crows build their nests in early April, so I did not expect to see mating in January. However, on a snowy afternoon in the new year I saw a circling male glide down to a horizontal oak branch and mount a waiting female. I looked round for a possible early nest but saw none; maybe the male crow suddenly felt in an amorous new year mood – after all, daylight was beginning to increase. Later that freezing day, I saw repeated matings, quite unsurprisingly, by a Collared Dove pair.

No longer, in winter, do I see Little Owls out hunting for beetles or earthworms in the late afternoon and I understand that in some Somerset farming districts they have quite ceased to breed. Even so, the Tawny Owl keeps its numbers and is the commonest owl in all our woods.[24] The hooting of the male can be heard, as song, through the year but it is commonest from February to May and again from August to October – when young birds are trying to establish territories. It seems, understandably, that Tawny Owls go hunting then and have little time for hooting. Tawny Owls, admittedly, are very nocturnal in their

24 A juvenile Tawny Owl in June. The young owl has just flown from its nest-hole and has found a good twig support. If seen by day, small woodland birds will gather in protest, uttering alarm calls.

behaviour and one does not often hear them by day. I do hear them occasionally by day, however, during the summer, probably when they are disturbed at roost. As an example, one afternoon in a Somerset plantation last June, I suddenly heard loud Tawny Owl hooting which was followed at once by a burst of alarm calling by a Great Spotted Woodpecker, followed by the owl vocalization once again. Although I could not see either bird, I suspect that a food-seeking woodpecker had approached a dozing owl too closely, so causing a minor altercation. It is to be expected that birds compete for food, especially in winter. Yet some do behave rather foolishly, at least by human standards, when a feast – quite artificially – is provided for them. Thus, a particular hen Blackbird appeared to put all her energy into chasing rivals from scattered helpings of oats in my garden; this greedy bird, having fed well, occupied herself in chasing off other Blackbirds, Song Thrushes, Robins and Pied Wagtails. Incidentally, one limping Pied Wagtail seen at that time, had a swelling, hazel-nut size, half way up one of its legs: was this lump the result of a fracture or the response to local infection?

Like some Blackbirds, individual Robins can be very possessive of garden feeding areas. Soon after dawn one day last February, I saw a Common Shrew investigating and eating oats and fallen peanuts but the meal could not be enjoyed in peace: a jealous Robin swooped to repel the shrew and, later, the process was repeated when the shrew re-emerged from cover. Of course, some birds like to feed on smaller birds, even in towns, and on a January visit to a Taunton store I watched a female Sparrowhawk surprise and then chase a small bird across the traffic stream. Then, during February, I happened to see another small bird, a female Greenfinch, flying at speed across a clearing with a cock Pheasant in pursuit. The Greenfinch disappeared into the foliage of a juniper bush while the Pheasant tried, noisily, to beat its way into the bush but, eventually, it had to abandon the attempt through exhaustion! Pheasants will readily eat carrion but I have never heard of one actually catching and eating a small bird.

In Somerset, people do not normally eat small wild birds these days but many of us enjoy cultivated mushrooms throughout the year. Nevertheless, we look forward to the autumn fungal season when we can pick our own field ones in suitable areas. All fungi are fascinating, whether or not we want to eat them and, usually, there are some to be found throughout the year. Last March, there were some fine specimens of Blushing Brackets growing on willows; the red-brown tops of the brackets, zoned concentrically, were particularly attractive when wet and reflecting sunlight. One could hardly eat those tough brackets but I was pleased to come across a very tasty large fungus on moorland last June. This specimen proved to be a big Large-spored Mushroom, which in due course made an ample meal of fine flavour. As I picked that fungus, however, I noted a coiled Adder on a grassy platform just above it. I saw that the snake was pale and freshly coloured and then I realised that there was a shed skin not far away: obviously that was the reason for the pristine appearance. The pallid colouring was brown with the normal black, diamond patterning; doubtless the snake was a female, which would agree with June skin sloughing. Sadly, the artistically shaded Viper slid away into heather as I unpacked my camera.

Brimstone butterflies, as expected, were in welcome yellow flight in good numbers in Somerset in March.**[25]** I wondered how many Painted Ladies would be about this summer (we all remember the great invasion of June 1996) but, writing now soon after midsummer, I have yet to spot one. But I was glad to spot several Holly Blues on the wing in April – they have been very scarce in recent years. During May, I noted quite a good quota of other well coloured butterflies: Speckled Woods, Common Blues and Orange Tips **[26]** but, of late, cool, cloudy June weather with rain showers, some very heavy, has not been encouraging for butterflies or for dragonflies either. Still, the common dragonfly species have been flying in their proper habitats and, early on, Large Red Damselflies were quite common.

In early May I was pleased to see the small and almost spherical nest of a Goldcrest in trailing Honeysuckle. Moss, sticky cobwebs and a liberal

25 A Brimstone butterfly feeding on a Dandelion; this is a female because of its green colouring – the male is a sulphur-yellow. This attractive butterfly is on the wing in spring or in late summer; over the winter it hibernates in evergreen bushes where, with wings closed, it looks very like a leaf. The species is common over the Somerset Levels where there is plenty of Alder Buckthorn and where the female lays her eggs.

26 An Orange-Tip in May. Only the males have orange tips to the wings. The butterfly is single brooded and only flies in spring and early summer; the female is white with a black spot on each fore-wing. The under side of the wings for both sexes shows greenish mottling.

lining of small feathers combine to make a cosy nest; there were so many feathers that the eggs were quite hidden, as is usual for this species. In late May I walked along the same valley and, to my surprise, the last of the Goldcrest young were just leaving the nest. One of the chicks perched conveniently on a nearby stump, so I was able to obtain a Goldcrest photograph to remind me of the occasion.[27] I failed, however, to photograph a coastal Peregrine, perched and well silhouetted, during a foggy springtime beach walk: the Peregrine co-operated; but the fog was too dense. One feature of last May for me has been excellent song from Garden Warblers. On the Quantocks, some nest in thick rhododendron clumps while others select dense Nettle and Bramble cover. Blackcaps choose somewhat similar habitats.

I listened to one Garden Warbler which sang beautifully from rhododendron cover in a woodland glade soon after dawn while a strident Song Thrush chose the top of a dead Hawthorn: the birds sang together, almost as a duet; this melodious combination was repeated on other mornings too. Some people complain of the difficulty in separating the song of Blackcap from that of Garden Warbler and, at times, it can be nearly impossible, for some Blackcaps are clever mimics. But, in

27 This newly-flown Goldcrest chick has just left the warmth of a beautiful, mossy and feather-lined nest, cleverly suspended from a branch. As Goldcrests lay seven or eight eggs, there is a tight fit for the nestlings as they grow; nesting trees are commonly conifers, high up, but, lower down, creepers may be selected.

general, there is no problem as the Garden Warbler's song is more sustained and at a more contralto pitch than the intermittent, soprano Blackcap. Calls differ too, with the Blackcap uttering hard 'tac, tac' notes while those of the Garden Warbler are, mainly, short rasping churrs. The Blackcap's nest is built of finer constituents than that of the other warbler and is provided with 'basket handles'; the sites are similar and commonly these are in dense undergrowth, including rhododendrons, Brambles and Nettles. It is noticeable that Garden Warblers use quite coarse materials in building their nests; indeed, some of the dried grasses utilised are often like straws. Many Quantock areas provide ideal Willow Warbler breeding territories and it is interesting how some cocks sing with greater frequency than others. While I was listening to one male Willow Warbler singing from a Hawthorn in May another male, evidently an intruder, appeared in the same bush: he was alarmed at with vehemence and, in consequence, flew off. The resident cock then began to sing with the song strophes almost continuous, although of a very low amplitude. Whether the intruder eventually returned to take over the territory I do not know, but there was fine singing from that clump of Hawthorns right through to late June.

There are scattered areas of gorse over the Quantock moorland and this summer several pairs of Linnets have used them as nest sites – quite as expected, some of you will maintain. Even so, a neighbour tells me that Linnets were common singing hedgerow finches in Somerset fifty years back but now there are none – at least, in the hedges near his home. Without doubt, Linnets have reduced in numbers in recent years, probably because of weed seed scarcity near villages and farms. Linnets, like Goldfinches, feed their young with regurgitated food; a Linnet does not approach its nest with a caterpillar in its bill, as will a Chaffinch. In general, I do not think that this year's breeding season has been a good one for the smaller birds. Heavy cold rain in June will have chilled small nestlings and insect food is difficult for the parents to obtain under such conditions. Furthermore, I see more and more Grey Squirrels about in nearby woods; they love egg or nestling meals and so compete with Weasels, Carrion Crows, Jays, Magpies and many other nest raiders. Still, I visited a Garden Warbler's nest in thick Nettles in last June, following a heavy downpour and, happily, found that the young were active and developing well.[28] The vigilant parents, understandably, called harshly at me until I set off on my homeward walk.

28 This Garden Warbler's nest looks flimsy but is really surprisingly strong because of clever inter-weaving of dried grass stems. Blackcap nests and eggs often resemble those of Garden Warblers; both species often build in thick Bramble clumps and nests can be close to the ground, particularly that of the Garden Warbler.

A January butterfly in Taunton High Street;
a Blackbird's interest in creosote; bird distraction displays.
Early 1998

January 1998 started with relatively high temperatures; indeed, one warmish morning on the Quantocks I watched a wintering Chiffchaff catching flying gnats before it flew off with a party of Blue Tits, while a day early in the month brought a most unexpected (and early) encounter with a Small Tortoiseshell butterfly in Taunton's High Street. Blackbirds proved early songsters this year with two in West Bagborough proving particularly adept at good sustained song early in February while the middle of the same month brought an amusing encounter with an energetic and inquisitive male Blackbird alighting on the roof just above the point of my moving brush as I was creosoting a wooden shed. The bird appeared to want to inhale the fumes, which was more than I did. After a few minutes the bird flew off, only to return a few minutes later – clearly a creosote addict. The Greenfinch population seemed particularly high in Somerset last winter and I recorded some eighty of them perched on power lines on either side of a preening Raven; periodically, a few Greenfinches would fly up and swoop at the bird which is an unusually bold gesture for finches, in my experience.

The warm weather conditions of February and March encouraged the early growth of fungi – with larger than normal fungal caps on dung toadstools and spectacular wrinkled clusters of fungal cups meriting a photograph. Tawny Owls, too, were active vocally early in the year, and wasted no time in securing their woodland nesting sites. I saw a young Tawny Owl at the entrance of its ash tree nest-hole in late April and by the following afternoon it was clinging to a branch lower in the tree, with its mother vigilant from a nearby oak. After darkness fell, the adult female flew and called vigorously in alarm as I walked by, but happily did not attack. I would not have relished a strike by the talons of a protective Tawny Owl!

The protective behaviour of parent birds merits respect. I am reminded of the efforts of a Pheasant hen to protect her young from my intrusion into her nesting area close to a moorland path. The female ran off, leaving twelve to fourteen wonderfully camouflaged (but very mobile) chicks which remained quite still; however, a few seconds later the adult began to call and, at the first note, the chicks dispersed at speed and disappeared under dead bracken. The adult Pheasant then approached me, clucking loudly, evidently attempting to lure me away from the young birds. In May, I experienced another distraction display performed, this time, by a cock Blackbird inadvertently disturbed as it was feeding well-grown young in the nest; the bird flew almost to my feet and then crouched and wing-flicked. After nearly a minute of this behaviour the Blackbird flew off.

Cool, rainy summer weather usually means a poor bird breeding season, especially for birds with open cup nests; this was certainly so for June 1998. However, hole-nesting birds, in the main, have better protection and this clearly applies to Nuthatches which can reduce the size of the nest hole by mud plastering. One Nuthatch I watched was high in an oak in an old Green Woodpecker's boring; the large aperture had been altered to one suitable for the smaller bird. Of course, many bird species use mud in nest construction and an obvious example is the Swallow; the nest is a bracket of dried mud, mixed with grass stalks and feathers. House Martin nests also require mud of suitable quality; indeed it has been known for them to be built of freshly-mixed cement from a building site! Blackbird's nests, also, have mud cups, later lined with dried grasses, unlike the Song Thrush nest which is left unlined. Crows use mud as well to strengthen their nest foundations; this certainly applies to Magpies, Rooks, Jackdaws and Carrion Crows. Such is the resourcefulness of the avian community, leaving the observer delighted and fascinated, with a sense of discovery.

Surprises are common with plants as well as birds, as with the fine, translucent fronds of the Tunbridge Filmy Fern which I encountered, for the first time, this year, on a walk on Exmoor – a new and quite beautiful find, as far as I am concerned.

Birdsong mimics: Somerset and Australia; *Little Egrets; House Martins swoop on a Hobby; a Goldcrest on an oak leaf boat. Later 1998*

Looking through my diary and referring back to the rather dismal and cool summer of 1998 I was surprised to note that I had recorded a Blackcap in full song in mid-July in a wood. I suspect that the male was unmated and therefore still singing, but there was an added interest because I thought that there were several fragments of imitation in the song sequence. Song Thrush, Robin and Blackbird notes were represented briefly – all bird sounds which the Blackcap would have experienced from singing neighbours earlier in the summer. I know that it is all too easy to imagine bird sound imitation. In a given song, ideally, possible bird mimics should be sound-recorded and the sequence listened to and analysed with care. If the Blackcap was, in fact, unmated, then mimicry was the best method of increasing the quality of sound repertoire. Certainly, with bird species, it seems that males with a wide sound repertoire are highly attractive to the females: the quality of song and hence, probably, the capability of the singer is what matters to a selective, choosy hen. When Blackcaps have paired, as normally happens in late April or early May, then singing declines. Good, loud and variable song does not advertise a cock bird in dense woodland where visibility is a problem: mimicry must add to sound variation.

   An obvious example here is the amazing mimicry by male Bower Bird and Lyre Bird species, in Australian forests of course. It should be remembered that these species spend a lot of time at ground level. What, then, of other bird species which live successfully in dense forests and do not have imitation in their songs? The question is not a simple one. Anyway, coming back to a Somerset wood, why does the singing Blackcap sometimes imitate, while the related Garden Warbler never (or very seldom) does so? Then, when watching singing birds, there is yet another question: why do certain species, and the Blackcap is an example, sing with the bill mainly open, while others such as the Reed Warbler sing with the bill closed? If one is fortunate enough to watch a Marsh Warbler in song, it will be seen to have its bill open for much of the time.

   In a late summer visit to south Devon. I was not at all surprised to see a Little Egret standing by, or amongst, a flock of some two hundred Canada Geese, perhaps I was a little surprised, however, to sight no less than four Little Egrets on Porlock Marsh, together with other marsh birds in August. This small, white heron is increasing as a British visitor and is becoming almost widespread in distribution. Of course, the bird is now breeding in England; I would think there is a good chance that nesting could be established at Porlock Marsh, where there are plenty of possible nest sites, in due course. Unexpected calls from well hidden Buzzards, or totally natural and undisturbed behaviour, such as Spotted Flycatchers splashing in a small pond in late August while another circles overhead, are always a delight to experience, while the high drama of mobbing behaviour provides some spectacular and thought-provoking sights and sounds. Examples include four bold House Martins swooping on a Hobby falcon which may have already been on a migratory journey south, over a Quantock valley; or fifty twisting, turning and swooping Jackdaws ensuring a Raven keeps on with its majestic flight and doesn't stop to perch on a nearby Scots Pine.

The summer months saw few dragonflies. However, Blue-tailed Damselflies seem to have bred well and in late summer, Common Darters were numerous on the Somerset Levels. Early September brought the pleasurable sight of a few Clouded Yellow butterflies in what was, otherwise, a poor year for butterflies, not least of all the Wall Brown. There were few grasshoppers too, but at least (come October) I had a sighting of a pair of rather torpid Speckled Bush Crickets with their long antennae. It is always a satisfying sight to see Somerset's bird immigrants and each autumn one awaits the usual flocks of Redwings and Fieldfares. Still in early September, and not far from Watchet, I saw two rather pallid Pied Wagtails but with dark cap and blackish bib separated; I concluded that these were adult White Wagtails over from continental Europe, and not young Pied Wagtails of the British dark form.

From my observations, fungi were not plentiful last autumn and Field Mushrooms were scanty on the usual pastures. Wax-caps, of varying colours and species, were, however, in good numbers in November on some Quantock grassland, and so were certain fungal spindles. It is pleasing to walk in mid-winter in damp, bare Quantock woodland where the occasional Woodcock rests in clearings on fallen leaves. There, often spectacularly, the Velvet Shank fungus with its handsome, sticky yellow-brown caps sprouts from dying trees; surprisingly, this fungus can resist frost and probably freezing is necessary to cause release of its spores.[29] Another fungus which can be colourful in winter and, perhaps, extend the full length of a big fallen trunk, is the Hairy Stereum: small overlapping golden brackets contrast well with moss-covered oak bark. Also, in late December, dog Foxes are marking their territories and scattered rank, pungent scent areas give evidence of this. Should you stray into woods at night, then loud rasping screams and wails tell of the foxes' activities – of courtship and of conflict.

In sharp contrast, on a mild and still November day, I saw a solitary Goldcrest standing on a large, inverted oak leaf floating on a small pond. A captivating sight, the Goldcrest pecked around the leaf boat and

29 Velvet Shank mushrooms; these grow in mid-winter on dead or diseased wood and even produce spores after being frozen. Evidently, Velvet Shanks, with velvety stalks, contain a very effective anti-freeze. These fungi became much commoner in England when elms were killed off by Dutch elm-disease.

appeared to be feeding on tiny invertebrate items; then, after about half a minute, the bird flew off. I collected the leaf but disappointingly, could not detect any remaining insect food. The Goldcrest's weight would only have been five or six grams, so it is not surprising that the thick floating leaf readily supported the bird. It is known that Goldcrests will occasionally feed from mats of vegetation floating on rivers, but this usually happens during cold, wintry condition, when the ground is hard-frozen. Goldcrests do not commonly feed at ground level.

One waits, listens and watches to see the events which spring and summer will bring.

Population declines; *Butterflies and Dragonflies from the Mediterranean; Hedgehogs and Moles. 1999*

If one has ever walked slowly along a deserted drove or sat peacefully in the shade of an old field hedge and listened to the sound of bird song in the air, the silence of absence is all the more disturbing. Granting at least some evidence of global warming, it is surely important to take notice of the presence and numbers of birds, insects, mammals and plants as we see them, both nationally and in Somerset. Without such evidence it is impossible to monitor population changes adequately, as impressions and anecdotes do not summate hard facts.

I was reminded of changes in bird populations in the Chew Valley Lake in November last. One of the species watched was the Ruddy Duck – a small stiff-tailed, diving duck with white cheeks and a darkish cap. This duck is really a North American species but one which has recently escaped from captivity in Britain and has quickly colonised suitable waters. The same species has also hybridised with the somewhat similar White-headed Duck in Spain. Also at the Chew Valley Lake, it was pleasing to note a large wintering population of Great Crested Grebes – a species which has fortunately recovered from the detrimental popularity of feathered hats amongst ladies at the turn of the last century. Less easily explained is the dramatic decline since the turn of the twentieth century of the numbers of Red-backed Shrike and Wryneck nesting in the county. Alterations in man's attitude to wildlife can have a marked effect on species numbers, and often in a manner which cannot be predicted. At present, in Somerset, there are thriving populations of Chaffinches,[30] [31] Robins and Blackbirds, together with good breeding success for Rooks, Carrion Crows and Magpies. In a way that is as yet little understood, however, House Sparrows, Spotted Flycatchers, Lapwings, Turtle Doves and even Starlings (all previously common) have declined dramatically in incidence in the past few years. Can anyone explain why Mistle Thrushes, Lesser Spotted Woodpeckers and Corn Bunting numbers have been so reduced?

Dragonflies have been in fair numbers locally in the past season although, personally, I spotted no rarities. Of course, a few years back, Somerset experienced a summer invasion of Painted Lady butterflies, which were said to have flown over from Mediterranean lands; possibly the 1999 abundance of Migrant Hawker dragonflies was of similar origin, and, like the Painted Ladies, the Migrant Hawkers I saw seemed in good and un-torn condition. As with many migrant insects, it was difficult to understand how, in fact, they could have flown all the way from southern France; perhaps erratic thermal currents had something to do with it. It will be of interest to look at Somerset Migrant Hawker

30 A Chaffinch nest which was built in low gorse near Wimbleball Lake. The nestling certainly has a good covering of down; I wondered when, or if, the other eggs would hatch but I was unable to return to find out.

31 A nest of beautifully marked Chaffinch eggs in May. Four young eventually flew from this rather bulky but artistically constructed nest; it was built from strands of moss and pieces of lichen, to be lined with carefully chosen dried grasses and rootlets. The patterns of the eggs have a camouflage value.

numbers for the summer of the year of 2000. I have been impressed, however, by the big number of Migrant Hawkers I saw in the Quantock areas in August and September.**[32]** Anyway, the last sighting I had of a Migrant Hawker for 1999 was at West Bagborough in late October. This dragonfly species needs lakes or large ponds for breeding and I was puzzled as to the origin of the insects I saw feeding above fields and gardens in late summer.

As for mammals, it is said that Hedgehogs are reduced in numbers and that fewer are being reported squashed on Somerset roads. However, I know that some were about in and around the Quantocks in the summer of 1999 as I observed black, thin cylindrical droppings; moreover, I found that Hedgehogs were triggering the security of my cottage at night. I have mixed feelings about Hedgehogs, they eat slugs, beetles and earthworms and flesh in many forms. Imagine coming across, as I did, a Hedgehog chewing, relentlessly, at a live Song Thrush which, sadly, had become entangled in a strawberry net in a garden. Was this defence, assistance or dinner!

32 A male Migrant Hawker photographed in August at Westhay Reserve. These dragonflies are often seen flying high in large numbers in late summer; they are attracted by small flying insects on which they feed and all depends on the weather. This is a dragonfly which is becoming commoner in England; at the beginning of the last century it was a migrant from southern Europe but now it breeds readily in local lakes.

While it is possible to enjoy the sight of good-sized populations of migrant Redwings and Fieldfares in the Quantocks, and see numbers of Little Egrets feeding at Porlock Marsh and hear the sounds of a Cetti's Warbler from a tangled Somerset ditch, there has been a noticeable and sad decline in the numbers of previously common Spring migrants in Somerset, in particular Willow and Wood Warblers. While Hedgehog numbers have been reduced in recent years, the same may not apply to the local Mole population. Last autumn, I saw a profusion of molehills over pasture fields and, annoyingly, in gardens, including lawns and flower beds. Furthermore, there is no doubt that moles are common in woodland; mole hills and surface burrows are present in glades and along rides but they are not easy to detect as they are obscured by dead leaves and decaying vegetation. Moles like rich, loamy soil, where they can burrow to locate their earthworm prey; Moles will not take to shallow, acidic stony soils. Occasionally, they will surface where they can leave tracks on suitable moist earth. I saw one partial woodland track recently, with two or three good impressions from back feet; the Mole's fore-limb has a big digging hand which only leaves a linear claw impression during walking while the underside of the Mole's abdomen will leave a drag line centrally. Quite recently, I removed a dead Mole found in a neighbour's garden. Both its body and fur was in good condition. I was, however, unable to discover the cause of death of this fine creature.

Cannibal Pheasants; a Herring Gull fight; foolish bird nesting patterns; a Buzzard in the sky with a snake. Earlier 2000

In January I saw a dead female Pheasant in a country lane, evidently killed by a passing vehicle. Standing by was another hen Pheasant which pecked at the carcass and was swallowing small pieces of flesh; yes, clearly some Pheasants do eat flesh and, evidently some individuals may be cannibals. Then, in March, just after I had creosoted a fence, a male Great Tit flew to contact the fence surface, touching it with his beak and fluttering to keep in position. That Great Tit had a strange taste for it as he returned to the ground and flew to contact the fence on two more occasions before departing. Curiously, this was just like the male Blackbird which came very close as I was creosoting before; was this another creosote addict?

At the coast, near Porlock Weir, I spotted two Herring Gulls which were each pulling at and tweaking pieces of ground vegetation by a muddy creek, with a rising tide, in mid-April. Vigorous challenge calls, with the head raised, were uttered by the birds; soon, the gulls attacked each other on the water, with each clasping the other's wings with its beak. The birds twisted and wing-flapped and, shortly, one had submerged with the victor on top. But the expected drowning did not occur and the underwater gull surfaced skilfully, with the birds flying off to trumpet aggressively at each other from a distance. Obviously both birds were enemies; however, as there was no obvious prize food source and the area was not a known or suitable breeding ground, I was puzzled as to the reason. Maybe the birds just enjoyed a punch-up? Yet a large Brown Rat which I saw swimming expertly across the River Tone in Taunton on a February day was well tolerated by a party of Mallards, when it passed through the centre of a group. The Mallards seemed quite unconcerned, surprisingly to me.

Another surprise observation involved Long-tailed Tits. Late in April I saw a feeding party of six or seven of these delightful birds in a Quantock wood. Now Long-tailed Tits are early breeders; normally, winter flocks break up during February, pairing occurs and first nests are built in March. The birds I saw were all adult, so they could not have been part of an unusually early family group (1999 had been a mild winter); so, I suppose, the mystery must remain. Another mystery to me is why a Swallow came to die on a moorland slope on the Quantock Hills. During a May walk, I came across a decomposing Swallow corpse which was being buried by Sexton Beetles. Sexton Beetles are rather attractive with their red and black colouring, which contrasted with the blue-black of the Swallow's plumage. Female Sexton Beetles lay their eggs deep in rotting carcasses, where there is plenty of food to be found by their young. Yet another bird puzzle occurred in June when I saw two adult Blue Tits fighting with fury on a path. It is almost commonplace for territorial Blue Tits to fight as rivals in March but, in early June, the birds are normally feeding well-grown young – either in the nest or when newly-flown.

I think that both Song Thrushes and Blackbirds have sung and bred well in the Quantock area this year and it is good to see plenty of young birds around. At a Blackbird nest I had under observation this spring I found the hen's behaviour rather surprising; when she was feeding her young she moved away quickly if she heard the call of the approaching male. When the cock had delivered his load of earthworms, the hen returned to feed her brood; maybe the hen considered that the cock should be encouraged in his rather infrequent feeding visits or, really, was she afraid of him? Usually, the hen of most bird species insists on feeding her chicks as a priority.

Anyway, in early January I heard good song from Song and Mistle Thrush, Robin and from Stock Dove on the Quantock Hills. The song of the Stock Dove is, admittedly, somewhat monotonous but it was quite a feature of certain wooded areas at the turn of the year. Far more variable, and musical, is Song Thrush song; although strident, some individuals develop some very elaborate cadences and long song durations. One Song Thrush which held a West Bagborough territory from January had a remarkable song output and sang almost from dawn to dusk: even so, I fear he remained unmated as no nest was built. Humans appreciated his singing but hen Song Thrushes were not impressed. Amongst butterflies, in February I saw a Red Admiral in flight during a warm spell. Was this a hibernator? If so, this must be a new trend depending on warm winters. To me, it seems rather fanciful to think of a Red Admiral butterfly flying across the English channel during February. Returning to birds, in late March I saw a female Sparrowhawk struggle with and kill a Wood Pigeon. I was able to watch the plucking of prey and subsequent feeding for a full half hour, before the Sparrowhawk flew off into the twilight, leaving me to assess the numerous scattered feathers. No small birds were spotted meanwhile!

On the Quantock Hills, Willow and Wood Warblers, although present, have not been plentiful this spring; Blackcaps and Garden Warblers, however, appear to be in good numbers. Garden Warblers arrive in Somerset later than Blackcaps and often move to higher altitudes. This year I haven't noticed any which remained to nest in rhododendron thickets, as I have noted in the past. The favoured haunts were with tangles of Nettles and Hawthorn or Brambles, often with Bracken growing in as well. I noticed that tall Nettles in June were often browsed from the top, so reducing nest concealment – I assumed that Red Deer were responsible. Happily, Spotted Flycatchers appeared to arrive in reasonable numbers this summer but the nests I have seen have been rather foolishly sited, at least in my view. To build nests in recesses in village street walls, where the sitting bird is repeatedly disturbed by passers-by as well as motor-cars, seems silly, the birds would be far more secluded in one of the several possible sites in my own garden!

Still, there has been plenty of natural life to observe in Somerset this year. I think Red Foxes have been more active than usual. They have certainly been vocal over the Quantocks and I have observed them returning from searching for sheeps' placentas and possibly, sickly lambs. In early May I had a fine view of a migrating Hobby passing overhead, looking like a large Swift; the bird had an amazing agility of flight. Perhaps equally thrilling was to watch a Buzzard overhead which was dangling a medium-sized snake from a talon; this was near Stogumber in early July. The prey was too long to have been a slow-worm so it must have either been an Adder or Grass-snake; probably the snake was being taken to feed a youngster – if it was an Adder, I trust it had been truly killed beforehand; an internal Adder bite would not be a pleasing experience!

Yellow Agarics; scanning earth-balls; *Robins' songs; dragonflies and butterflies. Later 2000*

I looked for fungi at Webber's Post on Exmoor one day in late September. Some fifty species were identified; somehow, I remember the occasion as a study in yellow, for that was the dominant colour of the specimens collected. The commonest species was one of the yellow brittle-gills; this fleshy agaric clearly had ideal conditions for growth in clearings near the thriving Scots Pines. Following this, the smaller False Chanterelle, also yellow, approached the brittle-gill in numbers; this attractive agaric, with down-swept gills, was widespread amongst the conifers. The False Chanterelle is not edible and sadly, very few true Chanterelles were located, so no return home with thoughts of a delicious Chanterelle supper. Another common fungus was the Branched Coral, attached to dead conifer roots or stumps; the tufts of orange-yellow branches are hard and slimy, with the colour often showing well against the moss of the forest floor. Yet another yellow fungus found was the convoluted, jelly-like Yellow Brain Fungus, growing from fallen oak and gorse branches. In the over-damp November, many colourful fungi were noted on the Quantock Hills. Certain pastures, which presumably had not been treated with artificial fertilisers, had good crops of wax-caps. Of these, the sizeable, greasy Meadow Wax-cap was the commonest, coloured in orange or buff, perhaps followed by the striking red or scarlet hoods. Also conspicuous, were groupings of White or Snowy Wax-caps,[33] as well as Parrot Caps; these Parrots have both green and yellow shades on the cap surface as well as the spaced gills. Wax-caps can be eaten safely, but they are smallish and the flavour is bland; while I have not heard of any poisonous wax-cap species, I think I would prefer to admire their structure and colourings rather than consider cooking them. Anyway, also attractively coloured over the Quantocks this autumn, and appearing in large rings in some fields, have been Blewits or blue-stalks; now, these fleshy fungi really are worth cooking.

Although it is certainly not brightly coloured, one fungal species I was pleased to note on a walk on the Quantock Hills in October was the Parasitic Boletus. On scanning a series of Common Earth-balls, looking rather like lost golf-balls, I was surprised to see two or three small, sponge-gilled boletus mushrooms sprouting at the base of each ball; the resulting geometric design was quite fascinating. Yes, these small boletes really are parasites: they will die if their host, the earth-ball, is removed.

I think one feature of last September and October was the quality of Robins' song. In some seasons, Robins seem to posture a lot at each other and, in other years, song appears to dominate. Of course, in autumn both male and female Robins sing and hold territory; song can

33 These autumn mushrooms are aptly named as Snowy Wax Caps, although they are usually over before snow is threatened. Most Wax Caps grow on unimproved grassland; this photograph was taken on pasture near West Bagborough. The Quantocks have several good Wax Cap areas.

be heard throughout the year, except when the birds are in heavy moult. Young Robins, hatched in April perhaps, will start singing in July, while still in their brown, spotted plumage, but I do not know whether both sexes are involved. For red-breasted adults, I believe that males are bolder and more inquisitive than females, so if a Robin approaches you closely and starts to sing, it is probably a cock.**[34]** Anyway, can you distinguish between male and female Robin song in autumn? I do not think there is an easy answer here; the female's song is said to be quieter and more wistful than that of the male. Then there is another question: how does the male's autumn song differ from that uttered in the spring? On listening to Robin songs recorded through the year, it is difficult to give a definite opinion in many cases. Females stop singing when they have paired; usually pairing has occurred by the end of December, so late January song is almost certainly from males. The Robin's melodious, complex warble has several phrases, each lasting about four seconds and made up of alternate high and low notes; necessarily, each song sequence is different. To listen to autumn Robin song, I suggest that dusk is the best time; most woodland Robins attempt a song before

34 A Robin in the snow, looking out for an open patch to find a worm or two; this vigilant bird, probably a male, will not tolerate any other Robin, other than his mate, intruding into his territory.

retiring to roost. Further, on a still evening, song counting gives an idea of the number of occupied territories in a given woodland area.

This autumn, there is plenty of beech seed, which is attracting Chaffinch flocks; those I have seen have been of mixed rather than one sex. Hawthorn and Holly has berried well, with plenty of food for thrushes (of different species) and Blackbirds. Last summer I saw young Peregrines which had flown from their nesting ledge; with adults, I have admired them in their flight manoeuvres and noted the skill with which they pluck their prey, methodically and relentlessly, if undisturbed. Buzzards have bred well; there seems to be an increasing trend for these hawks to gather in fields, both ploughed and of pasture, seeking earthworms. I have always considered that Rabbits are the main food for Buzzards; maybe some individuals are now specialising in earthworms.

On a walk on Porlock Marsh in August, I was intrigued by sightings of Fulmars over the sea; in addition, Little Egrets were observed on grassland. A small party of Dunlin appeared particularly tame, allowing plumage detail to be studied over several minutes; probably the waders were on a southern migration from northern breeding grounds.

I saw my last dragonfly for the year 2000 in flight in late October; this was a Migrant Hawker, a male, over the Quantocks. Dragonfly numbers have not been great in the past summer, but there is always plenty of interest when they are about. For instance, in early September I saw a male Southern Hawker fly to the base of a clump of rushes; it disappeared from view and, soon, I heard surprisingly loud beating sounds. After a minute or so, two Southern Hawkers, a male and a female, emerged separately from the rushes and flew off. Evidently the male had been attempting to seize an unresponsive female, which had been hidden previously from my view.

Switching to butterflies, I thought that, in general, they were in reasonable numbers in both middle and late summer and it was good to note several Small Coppers on the wing, following a period of scarcity. Commas were about too, but the main butterfly excitement for me (at least, one of them) was the appearance of Clouded Yellows in Somerset – doubtless immigrants from continental Europe. No doubt egg-laying occurred on clover and I expect that a fair proportion of 'yellows' seen in late summer were of English origin. Also yellow, and with the eyes, antennae and wings artistically coloured, or spotted in red, Brimstones fared well last summer. I noted several over the Quantocks in March and April and a lot were lured by Comfrey flowers later in the season: no doubt these were the summer-bred butterflies.

I cannot say that I saw a good variety of moths last summer and numbers, I thought, were rather scanty. I hope that breeding Nightjars, and bats, did not go short of necessary food. Certainly, I did not find that many moths had been squashed on my car, but maybe I had not been driving sufficiently at night. Even so, I was pleased to examine a well-grown larva (almost reptilian!) of an Elephant Hawk-moth in late September. I understand that several were spotted in Somerset last autumn, feeding mainly on Fuchsia or willow-herb. The well-defined red-and-black eye-spots, and the repeated protrusion of the front aspect, or trunk, of this large caterpillar as it feeds, combine to make this a memorable insect. If one wants to photograph the dark larva satisfactorily, then one must be careful that the exposure is adequate, to ensure proper details.

Foot and Mouth and closed paths; underwater Toad calls; thatched roofs; bird behaviour on the Tone; damselflies; competing sounds with birdsong in a village. Earlier 2001

Sadly, foot-and-mouth disease is with us. For myself, at present I am unable to walk on any common land, moorland or to enter woods. In consequence, this spring I have been unable to watch mating displays or nest-construction by Wood or Willow Warbers or even Meadow Pipits. Male Cuckoos have been in good song near my village but I have not heard a female, with her exciting, bubbling whinny; thus, it is unlikely that any Cuckoo mating has occurred nearby. This is unfortunate because there have been some most intriguing Cuckoo research reports of late. As, presumably, I shall see no young Cuckoos this summer, my own observations will be quite negative. Cuckoos are such enigmatic birds and fresh thoughts on their ways of life are to be welcomed. Anyway, it seems that the food-call of the nestling Cuckoo, on analysis, suggests sound coming from more than one chick, which must stimulate extra food collection by the hosts. Apparently, a single nestling Blackbird, about the same size as a half-grown Cuckoo, will stimulate food gathering experimentally by hosts by means of its begging calls, but the result is only enough to satisfy a small host nestling, such as a Reed Warbler. Furthermore, there has been a revival of discussion about the idea that young Cuckoos may, after all, imitate the calls of their hosts; thus, a newly-flown Cuckoo reared in a Meadow Pipit's nest may actually mimic the calls of the host. This is only speculation, but it is unlikely that much information can be gathered if one is restricted to gardens and country lanes.

Still, switching to amphibians, I was fortunate that I was able to watch spawning Common Toads in mid-March, in spite of interruptions by the flying in or the approach of vigorous Mallards. By day, I noted the marked colour differences between the sexes in several amplexus pairs; the small males were often reddish, with some being surprisingly pale, while the females were brown. Vocalisations were commonly uttered underwater, effected by pharyngeal movements (after air inhalation above); high-pitched release calls were frequently given by males and then there were their soft, rasping mating cries. Sounds were heard mainly after dark as mating activity increased. In daylight, near the pond, I saw a few heaps of discarded toad oviducts. Of course, toads are distasteful to many predators but when females are eaten the oviducts are often rejected. What had seized and partly eaten these toads? I suspected Mallards or Herons, but there was no proof; what about a Tawny Owl?

During February I was pleased to come across the small, circular bright-red discs of the Eyelash Fungus, giving an attractive colour composition on dark garden soil. Peripheral brownish hairs on the discs are, of course, the eyelashes. Also red are the red tips of some of the Cladonia lichens, which I normally see on the high, peaty parts of the Quantocks. This spring, however, I noted several growths of 'red-tipped match' lichen bodies on old thatched cottage roofs. I suggest you take your binoculars and survey elderly thatches in your area. It is surprising what can be discovered botanically, and, should you see clumpings of greenish, red-tipped stalks, it might be of interest if you can get a tame thatcher to obtain a few specimens for you.

Last January I was glad to note that Long-tailed Tit family groups were commonly taking peanut fragments from garden cages. This is a relatively new habit for Long-tailed Tits, which, after all, are not really tits but are in a genus of their own. Even so, in late February, just two Long-tails were coming rather than several; evidently family flocks were breaking up for breeding purposes – this is understandable as they are early nesters. It was good to see both Siskins and Goldfinches visiting peanut cages as well; certainly peanuts do attract many species and they are of high nutritional value too. Further, an opportunist, which now exploits feeding points in many Quantock villages, and no doubt elsewhere, is the Sparrowhawk. This wary and speedy hawk gets many a meal by lurking in suitable strategic cover near a bird-table.

Quite a good place to watch bird-life is on the River Tone, in central Taunton. In late February, I saw a resident Moorhen, probably a male, progress towards a Black-headed Gull and attempt to seize a piece of bread from its bill. The Moorhen not only immersed the gull but pecked strongly at its head: whether it actually obtained the food item I was unsure. Happily, as humans, we do not normally have to be so aggressive to get a meal, at least in Somerset. Yes, there is a great variety of natural behaviour to be seen in parks and gardens in springtime. Chaffinches, for instance, are common and successful local breeders. It follows that the display and mating behaviour of these attractively coloured and patterned finches can easily be observed near to home, maybe from a kitchen window. With a co-operative hen immobile on the ground, a male will alight and gradually erect its coloured feathering before dancing sideways with semi-spread wings, hence displaying its white patches; then, the showing of the cock's red breast really excites the hen, leading to sexual chases and eventual mating.

As with Robins, red is a significant colour for Chaffinches and so it is for Large Red Damselflies. In May, I saw a pair of these insects, with their black and red enamelling, in ring position over a garden pond, a pond already inhabited by a medium-sized Grass-snake. As far as I know,

Grass-snakes do not have a significant colour to which they react, although they are alert to any movement and, probably, snake patterns.

The weather in May was often cool, especially at night. I knew of at least two tit broods which perished in nest-boxes; I suspect that this was because of inadequate insulation from wood which was too thin. With insects, garden butterflies have not been abundant this spring. In April, on the southern Quantocks, there were reasonable numbers of Brimstones, Orange Tips and Speckled Woods, but I did not note a single Holly Blue – probably the larvae had been parasitised. After emerging from hibernation, Peacocks and Small Tortoiseshells, often rather tattered, flew well on the warmer days. Bumble bees, of different species, have been noticeable, particularly on Lungwort flowers; the earlier ones are, of course, all queens. Remarkably, I saw a small bumble bee in flight at midday at the end of January at West Bagborough.

Bird song has been a garden feature this spring, and not always just at first light. Some cock Blackbirds had original musical motifs, so that individuals could well be recognised. Of high quality too have been the songs of Swallows which nest in the village stables; last evening, in spite of lawnmower noise and roaring motor bikes, delightful, sustained, musical twitterings were uttered by four of these birds while perched close to each other on telephone wires. Obviously, one can watch and listen to wildlife apart from secluded moors and woodland although for certain species (always the most interesting), whether bird, mammal or insect, there is really no alternative habitat. For Cuckoos and warblers, give me the wilder Somerset expanses; this year one has so missed out on these, with no chance of discovering a newly born Red Deer calf. However, in 2001, I have not experienced the annoyance of being woken up by the irritation of attached sheep ticks!

Dragonflies; The spread of Cetti's Warbler; Cetti himself; fungi on Exmoor; Red Admirals' unsteady behaviour; a protective Tawny Owl; Peregrines and Rooks; a flock of male chaffinches. Later 2001

Despite the foot-and-mouth virus restrictions continuing, happily I was able to watch dragonflies on the Mendips in late June, even to having Downy Emeralds flying before me while eating lunch. Downy Emeralds are tireless fliers and glint green as they twist and hover in the sun; to date I have never succeeded in photographing one as they settle so rarely – at least when I am about. One tireless flier, and a really large one too, is the Emperor Dragonfly. As with the Downy Emerald, it is a beautifully patterned and coloured insect, with the male's sky-blue abdomen striped down the back by a broad black line. Having a longer flight period that the Downy Emerald, it was relatively common last summer over the Somerset Levels as well as Mendip. The males are very possessive in their territories; on one occasion, I think in July, I saw one fly out repeatedly to try and intercept the white, blown flowers of Common Cotton-sedge. The flowers were finally dropped when it was realised, presumably, that they did not represent a good protein meal!

During July, a few walks on the Somerset Levels, early in the day, demonstrated to me that Cetti's Warbler is well distributed there. This is a remarkable warbler, with the male uttering loud, warbling sequences, usually quite unseen and almost under one's feet. It can sing right round the year although springtime song is commonest; the utterances occur right round the marshy territory with the bird moving, quite invisibly, through the herbage. Yet, at night, when breeding, the male will sing from one position, although localisation is difficult. I have never seen a Cetti's Warbler's nest, usually in low herbage, nor the beautiful red-suffused eggs, but I have admired them in a museum collection. Cetti was an eighteenth-century naturalist, a Jesuit from Italy; probably he was active at about the same time as England's Gilbert White, curate of Selborne. No doubt, Cetti would have been delighted had he known that his warbler would move northwards in Europe in the twentieth century, eventually to be a regular breeding bird in southern England where, previously, it was quite unknown. For myself, I first listened to the warbler in Cambridgeshire a few years ago and I saw them in flight as well; however, I have yet to sight one in Somerset. Sometimes, in late summer, young Cetti's Warblers try to mark out territories for themselves; the herbage may be agitated where one bird has confronted another, associated with a few notes of alarm or aggression.

I enjoyed a walk near Webber's Post in September to look for fungi although it was very dry. Even so, the specimens were all of interest, including a few rarities. One species I hoped to find was the Parasitic Boletus; it does grow in that part of Exmoor but it appeared to be absent then. However, I was pleased to find the species in October on the Quantock Hills, growing in a peaty Birch and Holly clearing; I had seen it in the same area last year. The Parasitic Boletus sprouts from the base of the Common Earth-ball, and not from any other fungal species. Common Earth-balls, golf-ball-like, have a most unpleasant, acrid odour and are quite inedible; I was surprised, therefore, to learn that the Parasitic Boletus is an edible species. The fungus is a small one and several agarics would have to be gathered for a reasonable meal. Still, I would like to have at least a taste, for after all, several Somerset boletus species are delicious when cooked.

Last summer, most of the commoner butterfly species were present in fair numbers over the Quantocks. Of these, the Speckled Wood seemed to fare well and I thought it may have been perhaps commoner than usual. In late summer, there were plenty of Red Admirals over the Quantocks, especially round the villages and in gardens; they persisted well into October too. Unsurprisingly, decaying fallen apples attracted the Red Admirals, which fed on the fruit juice or, eventually, cider. Some of the visiting admirals became unsteady and irregular in flight, thus presenting an easy meal for a hungry bird. Flight must be difficult after alcoholic excess; certainly, one would hope that airline pilots keep to tea or orange juice! Once, in late September, as I put old, fallen squashed apples on my compost heap, a Red Admiral flew to contact my hand: I realised that what the butterfly really wanted was an alcoholic drink!

Moving to dusk and darkness, I noticed that Tawny Owls hooted well during October but appeared to be all silent from early November. In October, I heard good hooting in a certain woodland patch and, also, bouts of attractive, musical trilling. These trills are given by a male attempting to lure a female; the sounds may be heard at all times of the year but I think they are most common in October. Anyway, whilst listening to a vocal Tawny Owl in a grove in October, as darkness fell, a large bird landed in the deep leaf litter beside me. On turning to try and view it, the bird flew up, quite silently. Without doubt, this was a Tawny Owl which had landed only about two feet away from me. Obviously, I was an intruder, and female Tawny Owls, when they have young, can be very aggressive towards people. Of course, Tawny Owls breed in the spring and could hardly have any young about in the autumn; did that owl think I was something edible?

Still on the subject of birds, on September evening I noticed that local Rooks became very agitated and rose into the air, circling and calling with anxiety. Soon I saw the reason for the Rooks' behaviour as a Peregrine appeared in the sky, flying directly to the west. The Rooks, continuing to circle, were completely ignored by the falcon which was probably in determined flight to its roosting site; shortly afterwards, the assembled Rooks made off to their roosting trees. I wonder if a Peregrine would, in fact, tackle a Rook, with its formidable beak and claws, in mid-air? At the time, I noticed that small birds just seemed to disappear at the sight of the Peregrine. It is remarkable at the distance at which birds will detect an approaching falcon; if one bird calls in alarm and flees to cover the others will quickly fly in as well; assembled Chaffinches went into cover very rapidly.

Chaffinches bred well in the Quantocks area last spring and on one day in June I counted ten of them taking food in my garden. Curiously, eight of the ten appeared to be adult males and certainly not juveniles which had been hatched that year. Now, adult male Chaffinches do not normally associate peacefully during the nesting season and I would hardly think that it could be normal behaviour even in late June. The puzzle remains; a flock of adult male Chaffinches, even if they were non-breeders, seems a mystery at that date. I did not see the male Chaffinch flock subsequently, although there were plenty of young Chaffinches about with their parents.

Woodpecker drumming; Cocks' nests; *Cetti's Warblers at dawn; moth's wing amputation; a discarded belt. Earlier 2002*

I heard especially good drumming by Great Spotted Woodpeckers in the Quantock woods during March, but the sounds declined rather quickly, I felt. I detected very little drumming by the Lesser Spotted Woodpecker last spring and, sadly, the species appears to be getting scarce in Somerset. Woodpecker drumming is, without doubt, territorial advertisement by the male and the tone varies according to the woody site selected. Another related mechanical sound is made when the nest cavity is excavated, with wood chips landing at the base of the tree; then, another form of mechanical sound is made when dead bark is opened up so that woodpeckers can get at hidden invertebrate food. Perhaps surprisingly, many people still believe that the purpose of springtime drumming is to obtain food and, furthermore, many naturalists in the nineteenth and early twentieth centuries maintained emphatically that woodpecker drumming was entirely of vocal origin. All British woodpecker species have effective vocal call notes and the Green Woodpecker (which rarely drums) has a laughing yaffle as its territorial song; it is often assumed that this sound predicts rain but, then, rain is commonplace in springtime anyway. Clearly these woodpeckers, as tree specialists, vary a lot in their methods of sound production; the male Great Spotted Woodpecker always amazes me with the degree of loudness of its one second drum-roll – does it get a headache?

On an enjoyable May walk in the Wimbleball woods and on Haddon Hill, I was interested when I saw a Blackcap's cock nest in a Bramble clump.[35] Cock nests are not uncommon with some warblers, which build in bushes; really, they are vestigial, woven platforms. An enthusiastic, newly arrived male may construct one, or possibly two, cock nests; no doubt the aim of the male is to get an attracted female to use the platform as a base for a proper nest. Cock nests can be found especially in the defended territories of Blackcaps, Garden Warblers and Lesser and Common Whitethroats; I suspect that Dartford Warblers may build them also. Apart from warblers, the male Wren habitually builds well-formed and strong nests and two or three are not uncommon; the female Wren selects one and lines it with feathers before starting her egg-laying.

Earlier I mentioned Cetti's Warblers, which are now relatively common over the Somerset Levels; recently, I heard of one which was in good song over boggy land very near the coast. During May and June I was pleased to hear quite a lot of song phrases from this little-seen, chunky and resident warbler. As usual, songs have been uttered from marshy

35 The nest of a Blackcap in low herbage; it was photographed in May at Aisholt Common. The nest is constructed from interwoven, graduated dried grasses; not uncommonly, the hen will collect cobweb with which to decorate the nest rim, as in this case. Characteristically, the nest is partly suspended by basket handles from twigs; the nest is built by the hen but sometimes the male will construct a vestigial platform before a mate is secured.

herbage, with notes which are loud, penetrating, and sometimes almost explosive in quality. Often the warble commences with an alerting, high-pitched 'chick', very like the call-note of the Great Spotted Woodpecker; the same sound may be given in isolation also but probably only by the male in spring or summer. In the summer of 200l, I saw no Cetti's Warblers although I heard them on several occasions; normally they are so elusive and expert at progressing unseen through dense ground cover. However, I had good views of the bird on two occasions during May. Once a Cetti's Warbler, which had been in song suddenly flew to a willow branch just above me; I saw it in some detail before it dived into the base of a reed-bed. Then, on another occasion, a vocal male emerged from a hawthorn and uttered two high-frequency, trilled notes which, probably, meant alarm because of my presence in its territory; it then flew upwards and over me into willow foliage. My observations have been made at or soon after dawn so visibility has been poor; however, I read a report where two Cetti's Warblers were seen fighting on a path at midday. These birds may well have been young birds of the year, trying to get some land of their own.

Nearby songsters in the Cetti's Warbler marshy habitat are both Reed and Sedge Warbler. The Sedge Warbler is much the more attractive singer although, unfortunately, the male stops its song output very soon after it has paired; in contrast, the Reed Warbler will utter its rather monotonous song, with repeated phrases, well into August. Anyway, I really enjoy listening to a newly-arrived cock Sedge Warbler in early May; the bird will sing unseen from cover as well as in the air during a brief song flight. Often there is a remarkable outpouring, with a medley of harsh and musical notes and whistles; occasionally there is true mimicry and, usually, there are rapid variations in the speed of delivery. Perhaps unsurprisingly, this song is best heard soon after dawn and it may occur, intermittently, in the night.

Returning to woodland and village birds, it is always a pleasure to see parents feeding their young, whether in the nest or after having flown. One has to admire the innate skill of the parent birds. As an example, in early June I watched a male Blackbird carrying successive beaks-full of looped earthworms to feed well-grown young in a hedge nest. The Blackbird usually perched on a branch before going to the nest where it uttered a brief sequence of flute-like whistles. Remarkably, no earthworm was dropped during these vocalisations and, moreover, the bill was opened only very narrowly. Again in early June, I saw a male Wren seize a small, resting moth from a wall recess; the wings were pulled of and the body was taken to feed young in a nearby nest. It was the skill in wing amputation by a bird with such a small beak which really impressed me.

Probably we all like to be surprised when on a country walk. Not long back I saw what I thought was a discarded black belt on a grassy patch but, when I was closer, I realised that this was a black Viper, seeking some sunshine and warmth. The Adder soon made off, but when I came back half an hour later it was out again and, further, there was a grey female Viper alongside, giving a somewhat intriguing pattern. I understand that black Vipers are not uncommon on Exmoor and also in the New Forest. The Vipers were clearly not keen to be photographed, with the female being more camera-shy than her partner. Anyway, should one see a lost black belt on a heathland walk, it is as well to be wary before rushing to investigate!

Butterflies; Woodpeckers; *Shovelers at Chew Valley Lake and Woodcock on the Quantocks; Exmoor fungi; a road death; watching Adders. Later 2002*

This last year has not been a good year for butterflies, although numbers did increase in the welcome sunny and dry weather of September. Anyway, in July I saw the Ringlet population reduced by one; I watched a vigilant Tree Pipit, perched on a Hawthorn spray, fly with great agility to capture one in the air in its bill.[36] Somehow I do not associate Tree Pipits with butterfly-catching but, probably, it is not uncommon. I was pleased to see a reasonable number of Holly Blue butterflies about this season, both during May and August, following recent poor years; presumably, there has been less parasitisation of the caterpillars. Sadly, there have been few Marbled Whites in the limestone parts of Somerset this summer, but I do not know the reason for the reduction.[37] In late summer, with fallen apples about, I expect to note rather drunk Red Admirals, Peacocks and Small Tortoiseshells which have been attracted by fermented juice. This happened again this year and, in addition, two or three visiting Hornets also showed lack of co-ordination; Common and Red Wasps were about too but appeared to be unaffected by strong drink.

36 The Ringlet is on the wing in July; this photograph was taken near Priddy. Ringlets are unusual amongst butterflies in that they will fly during rain. Eggs are laid on grasses and the caterpillars hatch out in about three weeks.

37 A design in black-and-white: two Marbled White butterflies mating in July. Marbled Whites are flying in July and August; eggs are laid on grasses on which the caterpillars feed. On hatching out, the larvae go into hibernation for the winter; interestingly, the egg shell is eaten soon after hatching. The species is often locally common over grassy areas in Somerset but, as with most butterflies, numbers vary a lot from year to year.

Turning to birds, in late July I had good opportunities of watching a juvenile Great Spotted Woodpecker feeding with its supposed father. I was impressed by the young bird's large and very red crown patch, which was emphasised by a distinct black rim. The adult male has only a red hind-crown while females have black crowns only; I feel that one can only speculate as to the reasons for woodpecker head patterning and colours. Over the Quantocks, Green and Great Spotted Woodpeckers nested in average numbers in 2002 but, unfortunately, there was a decline with the Lesser Spotteds, which reflects a national trend.

Probably most of us are pleased to watch a Buzzard in flight and interest is added if a Raven flies to attack it; I was watching such an incident one day last August when, to my surprise, a Wood Pigeon, which had been in song, flew up as well to join the attack. Actually the Buzzard just flew on, without deviating in any way, and the Wood Pigeon went back to its tree and resumed singing.

A feature of a walk at Chew Valley Lake in October was the presence of large numbers of Shovelers, swimming in small flocks and uttering hard, grunting cries. The duck breeds in the area and drakes display in spring; however, the numbers seen suggested a winter migration and, no doubt, the reservoir is a pleasant place for the colder months of the year. A male Shoveler is a truly handsome dabbling duck, with its broad, specialised bill, green head and chestnut flanks. Drake Shovelers can have little natural camouflage but this is not so for Woodcocks, of which I noted several in Quantock woods during October. This long-billed woodland wader is streaked in browns, which blend perfectly with deciduous leaf-litter; it flies off noisily with a whirr of wings if disturbed. Robins are often woodland neighbours of Woodcocks; one may well hear a Robin singing its winter song as a Woodcock flies off. Recently, I heard a woodland Robin giving soft, intermittent hisses, which were interrupted by a few typical warbling notes. I saw no predators about and probably I will never know the significance of such utterances.

Conditions were very dry when I walked on Exmoor looking for fungi in late September. In consequence, there were few fungi about although three different *Cortinarius* species were discovered. The *Cortinarius* group is always mysterious. The agarics are often poisonous and, also, are very attractive in appearance; they should indeed be treated with respect. One fungal species which has fared well on the Quantocks this autumn has been the aptly-named Dead Man's Fingers, which sprout from dead wood; understandably perhaps, these blackened digits do not appeal to some people. Still on the theme of death, in October I came across a squashed Brown Rat in the dusk in a Quantock lane. A villager told me that he had seen a Tawny Owl swoop down to grasp and mantle the live rat but, unfortunately, a speeding car had gone over the rat and injured the owl. The badly injured owl was lying immobile by the hedge; most birds can cope with thirty mile an hour traffic but not when it is at sixty. Of course, Tawny Owls can normally kill and eat even big rats and so can several other bird species; a friend saw a Great Black-backed Gull swallow a rat entire.

Dragonflies have not had a good season because of stormy weather in early and mid-summer. However I have enjoyed excellent sightings of Downy Emerald dragonflies on the Mendips where, in June, some flew tirelessly over water. I have also had good views of the Red-eyed Damselfly, which really does have red eyes. It can be seen on water lily or pondweed leaves on ponds on the Levels or on the Mendips; binoculars are helpful in locating the insects on floating mats of vegetation. We should also look out for the Small Red-eyed Damselfly which has now arrived in England from continental Europe, with breeding having been proven in Kent; doubtless this will be cited as further evidence for global warming.

Perhaps I have been fortunate in seeing more Somerset Vipers than usual last summer although, in general, I believe that numbers have

declined, at least on the Mendip Hills. Many years back I recall cavers
near Priddy telling me that they regularly put Adders in their Saturday
evening stew. An Adder must provide a satisfying high-protein meal and
maybe a Buzzard realises this whilst planing down towards a resting
snake; nevertheless, I trust the Adder is killed before being swallowed as
an internal bite could be fatal. We first see Vipers on sunny days in late
April or May, soon after coming out of their hibernation holes. A male
and a female may bask together but often it is difficult to tell the sexes
apart. When fully grown, females are longer than males, perhaps with
an average of about two feet. We should not forget that adders shed
their skins, so colour shades must vary. Even so, males are greyer than
the brownish females; both sexes have a black zigzag pattern down the
back and a V mark on the top of the head. It must be admitted that
sexing can be difficult with some individual Vipers; I find it a useful guide
that the male's body tapers down to its end, while the female's is usually
much more truncated.

38 A coiled Adder – black form. These black Adders, male or female, are certainly not rare in Somerset and,
quite often, brown and black forms will mate together. This snake is enjoying some sunshine; it has to
warm up for full activity. Male Adders need warmth if they are to fight rivals or find a female; also, to feed
they have to chase after lizards, voles or perhaps beetles. To photograph snakes one has to approach very
carefully as ground vibrations are readily detected; they will not strike at one unless cornered.

Sometimes, early in the summer, two or even three Adders will chase each other, later to rear up in confrontation; these are likely to be males which are competing to mate with a local female. Doubtless, the female's scent acts as a stimulus to nearby males. Last July, on more than one occasion, I saw two or three Adders basking together during sunny spells and, intriguingly, some individuals were black.**[38]** In this connection, it is not uncommon to come across black Slow-worms in Somerset, although I understand that melanism is rare amongst Grass-snakes. With the black Adders, I noted that a darker patterning was present down the back; clearly, the genetic colour make-up is a complex issue. Unsurprisingly, one has to move very slowly to approach basking Adders, which can readily detect any movement or earth vibration. Adders do not have a hearing mechanism of the same type as mammals; they protrude their forked tongues frequently, sensing the air, and retreat at speed if danger threatens. They will not strike at people unless they are cornered but they will chase and bite their prey victims; Common Lizards, mice, voles and nestling birds are all eaten, normally after having died from venom, and usually underground. Earthworms are eaten too, but I wonder if a Viper would waste its venom on one? Some naturalists maintain that pregnant females, in July or August, bask alone, but I have certainly seen at least two of them together. The young are born in August or September. When I approach Adders I wear rubber Wellington boots and I have assumed the snakes would be alarmed by the scent; however, when standing still in a basking patch I have known the snakes to return, at least to the periphery of the site. In autumn, the Vipers, young and old, will move to a hibernating area, often a south-facing bank with plenty of mouse-holes. In winter, below ground, they stay torpid until they are warmed up by the spring sunshine.

Releasing a Chiffchaff; *Warblers' songs; ornamented nests; rooks and chimney smoke; spindle seeds; Humming-Bird Hawk Moth visitors. Later 2003*

As in 2002, one feature of the past summer has been the persistence of song by Chiffchaffs; surprisingly, in early July some males were still in vigorous song, at least in parts of the Quantocks and Exmoor. Of course, singing did decline then, but I heard more in September prior to migration. Chiffchaffs, however, do over-winter in England, at least on occasions; perhaps milder winters will increase this trend. I came across one Chiffchaff trapped inside a lobby window one June day. As I tried to catch the bird for release, displacement activity set in: the Chiffchaff pecked at dead flies on a sill and then made an aerial sally after a flying insect, with my hand just a few centimetres distant.

Compared with Chiffchaffs, Willow Warblers were not in good numbers last summer, and the same applied to Wood Warblers; on the Somerset Levels, however, there appeared to be plenty of both Reed and Cetti's Warblers. We have two resident warbler species in Somerset: Cetti's and the Dartford. It is good news that the Dartford Warbler is now present on Exmoor and the Quantocks, frequenting gorse and heather moorland. In spring plumage, the male Dartford Warbler is a most distinctive bird, showing its long grey tail, often cocked, and dark red breast with small white spots: it can hardly be confused with any other species. The male's spring song is a scratchy warble, not unlike that of the Common Whitethroat which itself may well be a summer visitor to the same patch of heathland. We know severe winter weather brings a hard time to any small bird; prolonged ice and snow could well eliminate Dartford Warblers from Somerset, and the results could be the same for the Cetti's Warbler.

Last summer, Blackcaps were plentiful and sang beautifully in most parts of Somerset, especially in woods with good Bramble growth. Blackcaps are not uncommon in winter nowadays, but these normally come from Scandinavia or Eastern Europe. It seems British-bred Blackcaps migrate south in autumn, although some may over-winter if it becomes sufficiently warm. The cock's song is an interrupted but attractive sequence of musical soprano notes. In his *History of British Birds* of 1853 the Reverend F.O. Morris gave a helpful description, at least for those days: 'Its tones, though desultory, are very rich, deep, full, loud, varied, sweetly wild and witching.' The brownish and rather plain Garden Warbler, a sylvan species like the Blackcap, also sang well locally last season, particularly in places with dense low shrubs and tangled vegetation. Garden Warblers arrive later than Blackcaps and often move to higher ground. The flowing contralto song is somewhat similar to that of the Blackcap and, in short bursts, can sometimes be very difficult to tell apart. The low bush nests of Blackcap and Garden Warbler can best be inspected through autumn bird-nesting, when leaf-cover is reducing and there is no risk of causing desertion. The Blackcap's nest looks rather flimsy, with interwoven fine grass and hair, although the structure is surprisingly strong and easily survives winter storms; often, there is ornamentation round the rim with pieces of spider web. In contrast, the Garden Warbler's nest (built largely by the hen, as with the Blackcap) is more substantial, its woven grass stems of larger calibre. The nests of both species are usually well concealed in low cover such as Brambles with Nettles growing through, but Blackcaps normally prefer a greater height than Garden Warblers, whose nests are sometimes almost on the ground.

Once relatively common as a summer visitor to Somerset, the Grasshopper Warbler is a skulking brown bird with dark spots on its upper parts. It may frequent marshy places but sometimes appears in scrubby dry habitats. The bird can run mouse-like through dense vegetation (like the Cetti's Warbler) and is usually identified by its reeling, insect-type, song which is very ventriloquial. Just why Grasshopper Warbler numbers in Somerset have so much declined, despite plenty of suitable habitat, is a mystery. Possibly there have been problems in its African wintering-zones or on its migration routes.

Moving away from warblers, one distinctive summer visitor to Somerset woodlands is the Redstart (classified as a chat or thrush); somehow I am always sad in August when it disappears from our woods. The poet John Clare called it 'firetail' from its frequently quivered orange-red tail. With good fortune, one may watch local Redstarts display in late April or early May, near a possible nesting site, perhaps an old fissured tree. The hen is attracted by the male's rather simple song of two short warbled phrases; if all goes well, the female will be chased by the male who will later fly in and out of the suggested nesting cavity. If the hen is impressed, she will spread her tail and mating should follow. It is well known that Redstart numbers fluctuate from season to season but the species was not scarce over the Quantocks in 2003.

Another common bird which surprised me recently was a Rook: one afternoon a cottage chimney was discharging unpleasantly acrid smoke when a Rook swooped to pass through it; soon other Rooks joined in. Did they get a thrill from this activity? Further, in late summer, I saw a Rook fly at a House Martin feeding peacefully high up. They grappled with each other before separating, the Martin flying off at speed.

Considering plants for a change, one rather scarce but attractive bush is Spindle.[39] Actually, the close-grained wood really was used to make wheel spindles and may still be. I know many of us admire the four-lobed

39 Colourful Spindle seed capsules; the fruits do not ripen until November. Seeds of Spindle are not eaten much by birds; however, they may be taken by Robins, Blackbirds, Great Tits, House Sparrows and sometimes by Long-tailed Tits. Spindle is a hard wood and really was used to prepare spindles.

red fruits which appear in autumn; they contain red seeds which have to be dispersed if the bush is to spread elsewhere. How does this happen in nature? I had a clue when I saw a Robin swallowing the seeds whole one October afternoon. Apparently, Robins disperse Spindle seeds either by subsequent regurgitation or by passing them undigested. The seeds themselves are poisonous but are surrounded by a nutrient coat known as an 'aril'. Certain birds will pull off fragments of the aril without eating the seeds, one notable example being the Long-Tailed Tit; the sight of a party in a well-fruited Spindle bush is one of the delights of autumn. Incidentally, while thinking of Robins, I saw one in mid-October posturing aggressively in a lane before a discarded red carnation!

Amongst insects, Humming-Bird Hawk Moths have been relatively common during the recent late hot summer. These are migrants from across the English Channel; they really do resemble miniature humming-birds as they feed, proboscis extended, sucking nectar from various flowers. I watched at least four feeding from Valerian, wings beating at remarkable speed. The energy requirements represented by their long flights and hovering for feeding must be considerable; all depends on the contraction-efficiency of the wing muscles.

I much enjoyed a walk at Charmouth in late September, looking at cliff formations and searching for shore fossils made the journey well worth while. Further, the occasion was notable for me because, while I was staring at a massive mudstone bulge, a Rock Pipit hovered before landing just in front of me. I was able to admire the bird's stocky build, heavy plumage-streaking and near-black legs (the legs of both Meadow and Tree Pipit being pinkish). The bill is very dark compared with the lighter tone in other pipits. Rock Pipits, usually cliff nesters, are sometimes chosen as egg-hosts by Cuckoos (not as frequently as other pipits). The eggs are flecked or mottled with brown or grey, not unlike those of the Meadow. In contrast, however, Tree Pipit eggs, in a ground or bank nest, show remarkable variation between individuals; beautifully freckled or stippled with grey, red or brown, they may be blotched with similar colour shades. Doubtless, individual Tree Pipit females have their own characteristic egg pattern and colouring.

I saw few fungi on the Quantocks last Autumn, due to the dry and hot late summer. However, autumn leaves have had unusually bright colours, some people asserting these never having been surpassed. This illustrates that leaf chlorophyll consists not only of green pigments: other pigments are red or yellow, as carotin or xanthophyll. The green pigments alone contain magnesium. Whatever the chemistry, autumn deciduous trees in red and gold were strikingly beautiful in afternoon sunshine, particularly Quantock beeches.

A Little Auk at Weston-super-Mare in 1848–49; an injured Peregrine; rescuing drowning female toads; a Dunnock at church; mobile slime moulds; a flexible Grass-snake. Earlier 2005

Winter should be the time to read books, and many old books give surprising pieces of information. Thus, the Revd Morris, in his *History of British Birds*, mentions a report of the nest and eggs of a Robin on New Year's Day near Exeter. That record certainly beats present-day early March nesting, which we attribute to global warming! I noted that Robins were very active in January around the Quantocks, puffing their red breasts and raising the tail to see off rivals and attempting to lure a mate. The Robin's orange-red breast is a really critical colour for the bird; indeed, I saw a Robin display at a reddish ember in one of my dying garden bonfires.

In another volume of the *History of British Birds*, Morris wrote at some length on Little Auks. The only Little Auk I have seen in the wild was one that had died on the Cornish coast during a winter storm or 'wreck'. Little Auks are small black and white birds with short, stout bills which breed in the Arctic and only visit British seas in the winter, feeding on plankton. Whether Morris had ever seen a Little Auk is uncertain, but I have my doubts. However, several Little Auk wrecks were documented in the first half of the nineteenth century, both for Scotland and England; one Little Auk was found dead at Weston-super-Mare in the winter of 1848–49. Many of us believe that the recording of animal, insect and botanical species started early in the twentieth century. Yet Morris, in his account of the Little Auk, was able to write: 'we may ... take pleasure in the thought that their having been thus noted in so many places, shows that there must be in each such case some one or more persons who both observe and record the occurrence of the birds that come their way.' It seems, then, that the value of records in natural history was fully appreciated in mid-Victorian times. Whilst on the subject of auks, Morris also noted that a Great Auk was found dead on Lundy Island in 1829, although he pointed out that the bird 'seems now to be extinct'.

I noted one January morning early in 2005 that the month was especially tranquil and Wood Pigeons were singing their mellow songs all round the village where I live; somehow, the cooing songs appeared to be particularly musical in the still air, and frequent too. Doubtless, early Wood Pigeon breeding is commonplace and pairs will often have two or three broods in the year anyway. Of course, Wood Pigeons (and domestic pigeons) are favourite prey items for Peregrines, of which Somerset now has a significant population and sightings are not unusual. In March, a friend rescued an immobilised Peregrine from the ground below some power lines; when I saw the bird it was perched on the top of a seat in a Land Rover and there it spent the night, after eating a little raw rabbit meat. Sadly, the falcon died two days later; at post-mortem examination, a broken wing was found, with spreading infection. I expect the bird had sustained its injury by colliding with a power line during a stoop. Power lines are hazards for large birds and, for the future, the effect of possible collisions with wind turbines will have to be monitored very carefully. In April, I was told of a Peregrine which was seen plucking a Moorhen in a field. I thought that a Moorhen must be unusual prey for a Peregrine, which specialises in flying pigeons but, apparently, it is not unusual during misty days when visibility is poor. Further, Peregrines will sometimes take young game birds on the ground as easy pickings, and even young Rabbits.

During last winter, several people complained to me that few birds were coming to their garden bird tables for food; I think the reason was that last autumn there was an ample crop of berries, such as Hawthorn and Holly, in the woods so there was no need to scrounge from garden hand-outs. Furthermore, Beech mast and acorns were plentiful and there was not much frost until February. January was a mild month, with a lot of early drumming by Great Spotted Woodpeckers and also early croaking and mating by Common Frogs. Some frog spawn was killed off by February frosts but I think some survived because of super-cooling; later, in March, there was another bout of frog breeding.

In March, I had good observations of breeding Common Toads in a deep pond;[40] the mating and male release calls had to compete with the sound of passing steam trains on the West Somerset Railway – a pleasant combination. As in past seasons, I was surprised by the difference in numbers between male and female toads; the small, aggressive males were so much commoner than the females. On a few occasions, I rescued females from drowning when I thought they were being kept under by overlaying by four or five competing males. But, had I left the amphibians alone, would the females really have drowned? I still wonder.

There were a lot of mice around in March; maybe there was a dearth of Tawny Owls. One Long-tailed Field Mouse was discovered drowned in an overlooked half-full bottle of milk at the back of my village church, to the distress of some people. Churches, at least rural ones, usually have some link with natural history; as one example, last December, a Dunnock somehow became trapped in my village church. The bird resisted all attempts to guide it to the open door and, instead, just flew upwards, quite out of reach. Still, the Dunnock must have been hungry as I saw it land on the top of a candle and eat some of the wax! Eventually the bird did find its way to the open door.

Certain January and February features over the Quantocks have been the rattling, loud and recurrent songs of Chaffinches, which have been

40 A pair of mating Common Toads at their breeding pond in March. The small male toads will often arrive at a pond at night, and already perched on the back of the larger females. Occasionally, a female will have two or even three males on top of her, as they struggle to gain a hold. Eggs are laid in strings, which tangle with pond vegetation. Toads are distasteful to many predators but they are vulnerable to attacks by rats and Tawny Owls.

dominant through to June. Chaffinches have been conspicuous this year, unusually so I feel, and linked with frequent chases and fighting between rival males. Quite remarkably, I heard a few bursts of song from a Chaffinch at the end of October last, although only on a single occasion soon after dawn. Then, in April, I noticed a singing male Chaffinch perched on a cottage chimney whilst bathing in the emitted smoke; as smoke enveloped the bird, so song amplitude appeared to increase.

As a change from bird behaviour, some people were mystified last December by the appearance of multiple, irregular, cream-coloured blobs which spread over the grass in one Somerset field. These strange patches proved to be the fruiting bodies or mobile (yes, mobile!) plasmodial stages of a certain slime-mould. This plasmodium soon disappears to give rise to spores; slime-moulds are surely highly mysterious structures. Presumably, slime-moulds (or Myxomycetes) are really primitive fungi.

I first heard a Cuckoo in song near West Bagborough in mid April, which I thought an early date. I first saw Swallows a few days later, which was a late date for the species for me. Even so, I think Swallows have been scanty in numbers and so it has been with migrant warblers, except for Blackcaps. Willow Warblers seem to have been particularly scarce. I understand that a lot of insecticides were sprayed in Africa last year because of a locust plague; maybe there is a link here with the scarcity of some migratory birds. Nevertheless, I enjoyed listening to a Grasshopper Warbler on the Somerset Levels in May, a species which is now generally scarce in the county; the strange reeling of the male is confusingly ventriloquial. Reed Warblers were in good song in reed-beds on the Levels but Sedge Warbler numbers appeared to be fewer than in the past few seasons.

Last spring I did not spot many Adders in moorland areas, but I had more sightings of Grass-snakes. One large Grass-snake behaved rather foolishly for its own safety; I saw the snake with its head and part of its body inside a small hole in a stone wall. No doubt it had followed a prey animal, perhaps a Bank Vole, into the cavity; this left most of the body exposed and at the mercy of any passing Buzzard, Fox, dog or even an anti-snake human. Eventually, the thwarted Grass-snake turned its head in the stone cavity and emerged head first, showing remarkable spinal flexibility.

I expect that most of us have appreciated Somerset's wild flowers in the past spring. Bluebells have been profuse and clumps of Wood Sorrel and Greater Stitchwort have been particularly beautiful this year in their Quantock setting. One bird species which has been noticeably scarce this summer over the Quantocks, has been the Spotted Flycatcher. This is often a confiding and attractive garden bird; I suspect that the species has had a hard time in its African wintering zone. However, one species which is certainly not low in numbers is the Wren; nests are seen in varied situations, including walls, ivied tree trunks, thick bushes and, sometimes just hidden in herbage on the ground. I brushed against the side of one Wren's nest a few feet up in a Hawthorn recently and, surprisingly, the head of a Wood Mouse slowly emerged from the side entrance! Yes, there seem to be a lot of mice and voles around and often I see them in daylight; clearly, there must be a general shortage of Tawny Owls, rather like that of Spotted Flycatchers. Sadly, the wet and cool weather conditions of early June are not aiding survival of nestlings

Sky Lark populations *and their sales in London in the nineteenth century; the Deer rut; butterflies; a Grass snake's eggs; Rooks ascending; Goldfish murder. Later 2005*

Just as many people in Somerset were disappointed at hearing so few Cuckoos calling last summer, so there was sadness at the diminished number of Sky Larks in song. Of course, Sky Larks still breed in Somerset, notably on Quantock and Exmoor moorland, but numbers round the farms have reduced considerably in recent years. Research has shown that the fashionable farming switch from spring to autumn planting of cereals is a big factor, as most farmland Sky Larks nest on grain fields. With tall crops growing on fields early in the spring, it is difficult for the larks to find nesting sites which are sufficiently open. Moreover, autumn-planted cereals allow much earlier harvesting, with stubble being ploughed in by September and this is no help for birds which feed on weed seeds in winter. Then Sky Larks which normally nest on grassland or pasture have also had a reduction in numbers; probably the early cutting of grass for silage kills nestlings and there is less cover to hide the chicks. Of course, the widespread use of herbicide and pesticide chemicals on farms must also reduce available food for birds in general. However, for the future, there is hope for an increase in farmland Sky Larks because it has been shown that there is a beneficial effect if some bare patches are left on autumn-sown cereal fields. If enough farmers, perhaps encouraged by subsidies, leave untilled Sky Lark patches, then there should be greater breeding success in the spring.

What is the reward? It should mean an increase in Sky Lark song and this is normally from late winter to midsummer; the male Sky Lark's song is remarkable too, with an output of continued whistled trills and chirps, uttered while ascending and when hovering high in the air, maybe almost invisible. It is notable how the Sky Lark population must have crashed in the past hundred years; thus, the Revd Alfred Smith in his *The Birds of Wiltshire* of 1887 wrote that in 1854, 4,000,000 larks were sold in London markets, with some 30,000 often being sent together. Presumably, these birds were netted; if netting for larks was carried out now, I wonder what sort of catch would be achieved?

Yes, winter is the time to examine old books. I can recommend the Revd Alfred Smith's book on Wiltshire birds, as mentioned above. It is interesting to find what he wrote about the Common Cuckoo which, as with the Sky Lark, is now relatively scarce in summer over Somerset farmland and around villages. Apparently, Cuckoos were abundant at Yatesbury in spring and also 'remarkably tame'; the birds were often seen perched on the author's garden railings, while answering each other with cries in different keys and were 'almost continually to be heard'. However, the author had noted some local reduction in Cuckoo numbers in recent years, although they were still 'very numerous' near Salisbury. I expect that the Somerset Cuckoos were just as numerous as those in Wiltshire in those mid-Victorian times. These days, I expect that most people would be delighted to have Cuckoos calling in abundance from their garden hedges, although a few might be tempted to reach for their rabbit guns in due course. Happily, we can still hear and see Cuckoos in Somerset, at least over the reed-beds on the Levels and on the heather moors. Some elderly villagers have told me that, when they were young, most bird-nesting boys had Cuckoo eggs in their collections; somehow, if eggs were collected nowadays, I do not think that the Cuckoo would be well represented. Well, with big changes in farming practices, the numbers of big hairy caterpillars have declined over the years and Cuckoos cannot thrive if they cannot find their favourite food.

It has been a warm autumn and this may be the reason for a late, and rather long Red Deer rut. On the Quantock Hills, I heard stag roaring in November, while mixed groups of deer were formed fully a month earlier. Even so, these early herdings seemed very peaceful; thus in early October I watched about forty hinds grazing with three stags, one majestically mature and two rather more youthful. The stags did not appear to be at all possessive or aggressive; presumably the male hormone levels at that time were below the critical concentration! Wet October weather certainly encouraged grass growth, so deer herds had plenty of food for their rut; perhaps surprisingly, the stags are said not to eat at all during the active period of the rut – they are too busy fighting rivals and preventing hinds from straying off for the attentions of other males.

The warm autumn has favoured some butterfly species; in the Quantock area Red Admirals have been in good numbers. I saw my last Red Admiral early in November and the last Peacock butterfly, for me, was in flight in late October on the Quantocks. On the Levels in particular, Brimstones had good numbers in the past year and were often seen feeding from Comfrey flowers. Alder Buckthorn is the main food plant for the Brimstone on the Levels; the plant has grown well this year and looks especially attractive in autumn with its crop of round black berries. I saw no Humming-bird Hawk-moths in Somerset last summer until mid-September, when one was feeding from garden flowers at West Bagborough; the insect has a very exact mode of flight, otherwise it could not obtain its flower nectar. Whenever I watch a Humming-bird Hawk-moth I wonder just where it had emerged from its pupa; some travel remarkable distances.

I usually see migrant Clouded Yellow butterflies each summer, but not so this year in Somerset; however, by the Otter estuary in Devon in

October, I met up with four or five of them. One moth I managed to photograph in May was the small, black-and-white patterned Latticed Heath. I do not recall seeing the species previously, although it is not uncommon and a day-flier. Then, to my surprise, I noticed another Latticed Heath over Quantock grassland in August; apparently, this distinctive moth is on the wing in both early and late summer.

In autumn, I saw several Common Frogs squashed on roads, with some surprisingly far from known breeding ponds; clearly the animals were dispersing while the weather was still warm. However, I was surprised to see a half-grown frog holding on to a low window pane on a November evening; the frog was viewed, unusually, from inside a room and I realised that one does not often look at a frog by its ventral surface. I wondered how the frog held on to a vertical glass surface – do frogs have sucker feet? On another occasion, in October, I discovered a frog, just about one inch in length, while I was clearing out a garden drain; I rescued the animal from a drainage pipe and it hopped off into vegetation cover. I assumed that the frog had somehow fallen through the grid of the drain cover; anyway, I was pleased to save a frog life that day.

On a walk by the River Otter in October I was certainly impressed by the numbers of Little Egrets seen. Many just stood by the river edge, elegant and slim; where there was a good view, their yellow toes contrasted significantly with the black legs. This small heron has certainly spread in Devon and Somerset in recent years; one would like to know where they were reared. On my journey to South Devon that day I was fortunate to see a party of Golden Plovers, some fifteen, which flew over a hedge close to my car; without taking my eyes off the road ahead, I was able to see the characteristic pointed wings and white axillary patches, so making a memorable car drive. Small parties of Golden Plovers are found in winter over Somerset farmland and, at the coast, as at Steart, Grey Plovers feed on the mudflats in winter. Grey Plovers are slightly larger than the Goldens and have black patches under the wings.

On a visit to the Somerset Levels this summer I had excellent and close-up views of Gadwalls, which are dabbling ducks of which I have had little experience. Evidently the Gadwall has bred well at some lakes on the Levels this summer, which is good news indeed. If one is close enough, the drake Gadwall is a truly handsome bird; there is a distinctive white wing speculum which merges to blue and purple feathering, while the breast is vermiculated and speckled as well, so contrasting with the black patch at the end of the body.

Like female Gadwalls, female Grass-snakes will lay eggs but without a hard calcium-rich shell. In September, a friend invited me to see a nest of Grass-snake eggs on his garden compost heap. Sadly, by the end of

September the eggs had not hatched, so there is little hope for any young Grass-snakes to emerge now. I believe there have been claims that Grass-snake eggs have hatched out in the spring, after over-wintering, but I would like to know the evidence for this. The white eggs were soft with a leathery feel to the surface and there was a lot of brown compost staining. I found that the eggs were adherent from secreted mucus; the coating is porous and water gets absorbed, so increasing egg size. Unfortunately, I fear that the snake embryos will die from winter cold.

One cannot watch snakes in the chill of winter but there are usually a few fungi to examine, some of which are frost-resistant. One summer or autumn bracket fungus which has grown well this year, especially on sweet chestnut, has been the Sulphur Polypore or Chicken of the Woods; when cooked, this is tasty with a sweet flesh. The fungus causes nausea with a few individuals so, if one is tempted, it is as well to sample a small piece at first. Few fungi were collected on Exmoor in September. The month had been very dry and the expected late summer mushroom growth was delayed as a result. Well, dry summers happen from time to time, as the chronicler Charles Wriothesley noted when Henry VIII was on the throne: 'No rain fell from June till eight days after Michaelmas', which was 7 October 1540. No doubt 1540 had very few fungi in late summer, when country people had to do without a bonus of field and woodland mushrooms to add some variety to their diet. For myself, I saw few Field Mushrooms last autumn but I found plenty of Wax-caps, which are now nationally scarce, on local grassland. Unimproved Quantock pastures, and some lawns, are good places to look for autumn Wax-caps. Red, orange, yellow and white species occur; exact identification is rarely simple but the agarics are excellent subjects for colour photography.

Also particularly attractive in Somerset this autumn have been the seed-heads of Traveller's Joy, with their varied silvery and silken curved designs. Amongst berries, the red clumps of Guelder rose have ripened well and so, as usual, have the black, round berries of Common Elder. Guelder rose berries stay on the bush until well into December when birds start to take them, and then only in really cold weather. Blackbirds and Song Thrushes are most likely to eat Guelder berries. In October, after looking at a well-berried Guelder bush, I looked up at a blue sky to see some fifty Rooks circling high over the Quantocks when, suddenly, about twenty of the birds separated themselves from the group and began to ascend in narrow spirals. Soon, the ascending Rooks were almost lost to view. Maybe the Rooks ascended in celebration of their powers of flight; after all, a Sky Lark will ascend as though in celebration of its song.

Returning to the ground, perhaps one could end with a puzzle in a Quantocks garden, in November. A small heap of goldfish was found one morning by a pond, with each fish having a chewed head and, next morning, this was repeated. What was the culprit? Herons, Mink or Otters would have eaten the fish direct or left them whole while Tawny Owls or Carrion Crows would at least have pecked or torn at the body. I can only suggest a fish-liking cat or rat. I believe that the garden owner believes that a well-fed, destructive cat did the damage; still, there is no proof for this and no more fish have been landed.

Hornets and central heating; *a deserted rookery; nest building and recycling; the three pairs of Pondskaters' legs; a Blackbird and a Rabbit. Earlier 2006*

The winter of 2005/6 was a cold one, and a dry one too. Cold winter weather conditions may be bad for one's chilblains but, often, the chances of watching interesting bird behaviour are increased. Anyway, one winter's day, with snow in the offing, I saw a Pied Wagtail hovering before an orb web below the eaves of a village cottage; no doubt, the bird was attempting to pick off trapped invertebrate food items, and not very successfully either. However, the wagtail eventually managed to seize part of the cobweb in its bill, pulling away most of it, and then flew to perch at the edge of the cottage roof where the cobweb was swallowed entire. Presumably, the wagtail had an invertebrate meal and, probably, the silk web was regurgitated later as a pellet. Cobweb-swallowing must be unusual for birds but I have seen it previously; I recall the juvenile Green Woodpecker which I saw tear at and swallowing a large web, doubtless getting a good meal from trapped insects and, maybe, a spider as well.

One large insect I saw walking over my cottage floor in December was a queen Hornet which I suppose had become lively because of central heating. Queen Hornets are certainly beautifully marked and coloured insects,[41] and I saw several of them over the Quantocks in May, no

41 A queen Hornet after awakening from winter hibernation; all the males and workers from the colony will have died off but the queen will have been fertilised, so the species can continue. The background stone here has a pleasing mixture of lichens; note the black dots which are spore-producing structures.

doubt searching for nest sites; it seemed that the insects survived the winter well.

The Hornet's golden-yellow patterning might remind one of the Goldcrest, which was common in Quantock woodland last winter. Goldcrests are attractive birds to watch as they feed, usually high in conifers, taking small spiders or insects from the foliage. Yet Goldcrests sometimes feed on the ground, especially in cold winter weather; one female, probably the same individual, often flew to feed on the ground below a suspended peanut feeding cage in my garden. I noticed that the Goldcrest only arrived when other birds, usually Blue, Great or Coal Tits, were actively feeding from the nuts; doubtless, the dropped peanut fragments represented good oil-rich food for the Goldcrest. The Goldcrest did not attempt to take peanut peckings direct from the nut cage.

The cold winter did not prevent birds from carrying out preliminary pairing or courtship displays, as was shown by a male and female Pied Wagtail on one December morning. I was watching a solitary male Pied Wagtail eating a food scrap on the ground when a female Pied Wagtail flew in to land nearby. Very quickly, the female wagtail elevated the tail almost vertically on four occasions; in response, the male bird raised its tail two or three times and briefly bowed the head. The female wagtail then attempted to feed near the male but, on this occasion, her presence was clearly not appreciated. Ungraciously, the male attacked the female, forcing her to fly off; the behaviour suggested that the birds were already loosely paired, with the female carrying out an act of appeasement, although the expected wing-quivering was lacking.

Winter bird visitors were around on the Quantock Hills well into March. In February I saw the occasional Woodcock in local woods, normally resting in leaf-litter by day, and unseen until the disturbed bird flies off with a clutter of wings. However, I put up one Woodcock which was not concealed on the forest floor; to my surprise, it flew off from a low horizontal branch of a Holm Oak in a clearing as I approached. Then, as expected, parties of Fieldfares and of Redwings roamed Somerset last winter, but I did not note large numbers. Yet Redwings can occur in enormous numbers in England; as an example, I recently came across one such account in a bird journal. Apparently, on an October day in Cheshire last year, about 145,000 Redwings were seen flying to the north-east; the birds moved in flocks of about five hundred, but where they landed up seems to have been a mystery. The Redwings must have been newly arrived migrants and probably from Scandinavia; maybe there was a later unseen re-orientation. Possibly, some of those Redwings eventually wintered in Somerset, or did they mostly perish over the high seas?

February was certainly a cold month but, even so, numerous mole-hills continued to appear in pasture fields, and on garden lawns too. I saw one Mole squashed on a road in early February so this one, at least, was on the move above ground at that time. It is not unusual to find mole bones in the pellets of Tawny Owls, so the animals probably travel on the ground, mainly at night, more often than is generally realised.

Also in February the local, hardy Rooks started to nest-build and some continued to stick-carry at the height of a snow storm; elderly villagers tell me that Rooks have always used this rookery, as long as they can remember. As usual, in due course, I found dropped half egg-shells, as chicks hatched, and watched adult Rooks arriving to feed small young. Then, in mid-April, when the noise of the active Rookery had been at high pitch, all fell silent. The rookery was suddenly deserted with young birds, and perhaps some unhatched eggs remaining in the nests. What had caused this mass desertion? There had been no shooting at the rookery and no obvious gross disturbance; it is known that Rooks will sometimes change the site of their rookery, but it is surely very unusual for desertion to occur before the young have flown. The mystery remains; the normal caws and trumpeting sounds of the rookery in April were sadly missed by people living nearby.

In March, Great Spotted Woodpeckers usually excavate their nest cavities, and some Nuthatches will select ready-made cavities for their nests. Just a few Great Spotted Woodpeckers will make use of previously excavated holes, as happens with Nuthatches, but are these birds at a disadvantage? If a tree-hole nest, or an open nest, is reused there is a build-up of blood-sucking arthropods, which must have an adverse effect on chick growth and development. Nest-building means a lot of hard work for birds, usually the female, so it is not surprising that if a nest is deserted some of the materials may be recycled. One example is the Long-tailed Tit, where feathers from an old nest lining may be carried for the construction of a new one, and essential spider silk is often reused as well. Chaffinches also will recover silk cocoons from a deserted nest; the nest is a beautiful mossy structure and spider silk is necessary in keeping moss fibres stuck together. Chaffinches are single brooded, but where there has been nest predation, the birds usually persevere until a clutch is reared.

The breeding of amphibians was delayed in the cold winter, as expected. Common Frogs which croaked and mated back in late January or February had their spawn frozen and killed in many cases. Still, there was a later breeding period for many frogs, with varying degrees of success. Common Toads in this area traveled to their breeding ponds in late rather than early March. As usual, there appeared to be a surplus of male toads in the pond I observed; breeding seemed brief and was over in five or six days, with plenty of long egg strings resulting to ornament the pond vegetation. One dead Common Toad female I came across had had her skin 'turned inside out', and her oviducts discarded. What had carried out this inversion and presumably had eaten much of the inside? I suspected a Red Fox, which will treat a Hedgehog similarly, although I suppose a Badger could have been the overnight culprit.

At this time, in late March, a walk by the Taunton Canal can be rewarding because of the variety of gull species to be seen there. One afternoon I noted several Lesser Black-backed Gulls; interestingly, some of these (all in adult plumage) had near-black upper-parts while others showed slate-grey wings. Scandinavian Lesser Black-backed Gulls, as a sub-species, have dark wings and birds of Western Europe show slate-grey ones. Many Lesser Black-backed Gulls winter as far south as West Africa, so the March Taunton gulls could have been on the move, migrating back to their breeding haunts.

There have been noteworthy displays of yellow flowers this springtime, particularly in late April. Some fields seemed to be almost covered with Dandelions, and buttercups have been nearly as profuse in some parts of Somerset; I am uncertain as to the value of the pasture to the farmer in these cases. Mature Dandelion flowers are a great lure for Brimstone butterflies, with both male and female relishing the nectar. But the yellow flower I have most admired has been the Kingcup or Marsh Marigold, both by Quantock ponds and streams and over the Levels. Then, in June, lakesides have been yellow with the Flag Iris.

I visited the Waldegrave Pool on the Mendip Hills in June, my first visit for 2006. I had been told that herbicide had been used to control choking water weeds, so I was somewhat apprehensive to see what effect the chemicals had had on the dragonfly population. I saw seven different dragonfly species in flight, mostly in reasonable numbers, so that was encouraging for early June; moreover, there was much more open water than in the previous season. But a brief observation period will not necessarily give the full story, and more time is really needed before drawing final conclusions.

One pond invertebrate which might have been affected by the herbicide is the Common Pondskater, a water bug, and an insect which will rapidly colonise new ponds. Pondskaters have three pairs of legs, as insects, and are rowed along the water surface by the middle pair, usually surprisingly speedily too; the front legs seize prey and the back pair is used for steering. The legs and feet are waxed by secretions and also they are very hairy. As a result, the insect is supported on the 'skin' of the water. In summer, Pondskaters have a meat diet, feeding on insects which, by chance, land on the water or have started to drown there. Pondskaters communicate by drumming with their legs on water,

42 A Cuckoo nestling alone in the nest of a Meadow Pipit on Exmoor; it will have the undivided attention of two doting foster parents. Sometimes, after leaving the nest, its persuasive calls will lead it to be fed by other passing birds! Clearly, the sight of that large orange red gape is a very compelling one to small birds.

so attracting mates or warning rivals; the sounds can be detected using an underwater microphone – that is if you possess one! Young Pondskaters hide in pondside vegetation until they mature; by the autumn the skaters have normally grown wings and can fly about searching for fresh waters. Thus, if you want your new garden pond populated by skaters, make sure that it is ready by the autumn as the insects become flightless in the spring.

Reverting to birds, I heard my first Chiffchaff in song on the Quantocks in late March, which was certainly not an early date. It seems that Chiffchaff numbers have been sparse in parts of Somerset this year; I fear that the birds have fared badly in their wintering zones in Africa or during migration. Cuckoos too have been scarce around Quantock villages or over farmland, although they appear plentiful over the reed-beds of the Levels or on the Quantock and Exmoor moorlands.**[42]** I have heard plenty of competitive Cuckoo song on the Levels where Reed Warblers are parasitised; this has included 'gawking', meaning gruff, bark-like sounds which are probably warnings by male Cuckoos to intruders. Some Somerset villagers have been concerned at the dearth of Cuckoo numbers, so different from the situation just a few years back. One wonders as to the reason for the farmland Cuckoo shortage. There seem to be plenty of Dunnocks around,**[43] [44]** as the main Cuckoo fosterers around the villages; possibly, it is the shortage of Cuckoo food (hairy caterpillars) which is to blame.

Anyway, Blackbirds are certainly abundant in the Somerset countryside, even allowing for all those squashed on the roads, together with the equally abundant Rabbits. Of course, our resident cock Blackbirds are highly territorial and many garden Blackbirds seem to guard their territories right through the winter. Small Blackbird flocks are often seen in Somerset in winter, but many of these birds are of central European origin, and will return there in spring. Last May I saw a village Blackbird which would not tolerate the presence of a small Rabbit; the bird swooped at a half-grown Rabbit and, pecking at its head and body,

43 The mossy nest of a Dunnock (or Hedge Accentor) in a low Bramble clump on Aisholt Common in June. The sky-blue colouring makes these eggs amongst the most beautiful of all British birds. This is a bird species where a great deal of promiscuity seems to go on; at many nests the young may be fed by three adults. Cuckoos may victimise Dunnocks which make excellent fosterers; strangely, the hen Cuckoo's whitish, mottled egg does not match the uniform blue of the host in any way. Yet, in Germany, the eggs of Cuckoos which parasitise Redstarts are a uniform blue and do match those of the host bird.

44 Three eight to nine-day-old Dunnock nestlings, together with an infertile egg, in a picturesque, mossy nest. Black tongue spots are all part of the gape picture for Dunnocks and the sight of them, as a releaser, goads the parents into flying off to search for more and more food. A gaping mouth in the nest is a compelling signal for a parent bird.

forced it to retreat into the cover of a hedge. I watched this behaviour in a lane, but I know some people who would be glad to have such a Blackbird resident in their garden!

Reed Warblers' nests; *a fallen nest; a Sparrowhawk swoops on a human; hissing swans; dragonfly territories; a Curlew gulps down a frog; autumn mushrooms. Later 2006*

There are several bird species which have second brood nests in Somerset, and one example is the Reed Warbler. In early July, by a lake reed-bed on the Levels, I was interested to watch a female Reed Warbler, closely shadowed by the male, pulling off peelings of dead willow bark and carrying them, repeatedly, into a dense willow clump which was surrounded by water. The nests of Reed Warblers are unique structures, being cylinders of dried grasses, moss pieces and reed flowers, and woven round three or four reed stems a metre or so above the water surface; inside the deep cup, the nest is completed by a smooth lining of reed flowers and feathers. Even in strong winds, the depth of the nest cup normally ensures that eggs or nestlings do not fall out on tilting. Clearly, the Reed Warbler I watched was preparing a second brood nest; hopefully, the first brood young were already strong on the wing. The use of substantial amounts of willow bark peelings must be unusual for a Reed Warbler; I would certainly have liked to have inspected the completed nest.

Also in early July, I was asked to see a Tawny Owl which had become trapped in a mesh of plastic garden netting, and had been snapped at by two aggressive small dogs. With some help, I managed to free the owl which was a young bird of the year. I thought the owl was dead as it just lay on its side on the ground, but eventually it revived and I was able to place it in a secluded hollow on a hedge bank. By nightfall, the owl had gone; one hopes it went off on a successful hunting trip after its ordeal. Doubtless, the owl had been severely frightened by the two dogs, even though it had not been injured physically. Feigning death does happen with birds; parents may try to lure predators away from young by distraction displays and, probably, the feigning of death can be an extreme and unusual form of this. Of course, the adolescent owl was on its own, and I saw it in an understandable state of mental shock.

But frightening experiences do not necessarily send young birds into shock. Later last July, I came across a domed and mossy Wren's nest on its side on the ground and, to my surprise, there were fledglings inside, while the parents fussed and alarmed in nearby bushes. Obviously the nest had not been properly secured; I soon saw that the original site had been in a smooth conifer fork at height of about two and a half metres. On righting the fallen nest, young Wrens (I think there were four) just cascaded out and dispersed at speed into neighbouring herbage. Certainly I saw no evidence of mental shock with those active Wren chicks, which appeared to be well-feathered and reasonably mature.

With their parents around to guard and feed them, I felt that the young Wrens had every chance of survival, although had the nest fallen a few days previously the birds would probably have been too immature for successful rearing. The moral for Wrens must be to fix the nest with great care should a tree fork site be selected. Then, in early August, I was walking in a Quantocks lane when I found my way blocked by a Land Rover. Whilst wondering if the female driver was in difficulties, I soon saw the reason for her stopping mid-lane. About two metres ahead of the vehicle a female Sparrowhawk was boldly plucking a Wood Pigeon; the driver told me that she had watched the kill as she was driving along. After another minute or so, the hawk flew off carrying much of its victim by a talon; no doubt some young Sparrowhawks, depending on their parents, were voracious for a meat meal. Evidently Sparrowhawks are becoming more trusting where people are concerned; certainly they are increasingly exploiting garden bird-tables. Indeed, a friend told me that as he approached his bird-table one day a Sparrowhawk (I think a male) was diverted in a swoop and, to correct its direction, landed briefly on his head! Undramatically, no harm resulted!

Yes, Sparrowhawk numbers are being maintained at a level which is higher than some country people would wish, but must be limited by available prey items. Tits appear to be in good numbers over the Quantocks, and Blue and Great Tits seem to have bred well last spring, although nesting outcome was thought to be poor for some parts of Britain. Unfortunately however, some migrant warbler species have been in low numbers; examples are Wood and Willow Warblers and, locally, I think, Chiffchaffs and Garden Warblers. As noted last year, few Cuckoos were heard in 2006 round Somerset farms or villages, and Swallow and House Martin populations appear to have declined also. Nevertheless, Blackcaps have sung well over the Quantocks during the summer, even including several unmated males; and, further, with a contrast in size and habitat, Mute Swans have been quite abundant, at least over the Somerset Levels, with many successful cygnet broods. Indeed, the hisses of protective parent Mute Swans were some of the characteristic summer sounds of the Levels during the past season. Without doubt, a fierce, prolonged hiss from a cob Mute Swan can be very intimidatory![45] Furthermore, last summer there were a lot of non-breeding Mute Swans about as well as the nesting ones, so there was plenty of snorting and grumbling Mute Swan sound at many lakeside locations. Mute Swans are often far from being mute.

The hot late summer evidently suited dragonflies in general. A speciality of the hill streams of the Quantocks is the handsome Golden-ringed Dragonfly and the summer weather conditions were certainly to its liking. I watched several of these attractive insects flying up and down

45 The two cygnets here are anxious to keep up with their mother who is probably moving to a new feeding area. Mute Swans feed on a variety of water vegetation. The Somerset Levels, where this photograph was taken, has a large nesting population of swans as well as high numbers of non-breeding ones. It is fascinating to hear the musical sound of the wing beats as Mute Swans fly overhead.

one hill stream just above the water surface; one of the males patrolled a stream length of about twenty metres while, lower down, another was maintaining his right to his portion of water. The insects would fly round me as I watched and readily flew under stream vegetation, which had been pushed over by cattle and formed a flimsy bridge. After around ten minutes of continuous flight, the Golden-rings would suddenly fly high and then disappear up-stream; perhaps they needed a change of scene or merely a rest. Another large Somerset dragonfly which patrols its territory in summer is the Southern Hawker; males will fly strongly about a metre above the ground or over water and patrol some forty to fifty metres of the side of a slow-flowing river or pond. These hawkers are very inquisitive and will come to investigate any intruder. Occasionally an aggressive Southern Hawker will attack an intruding dragonfly with such force that quite a knock is heard; also, a favoured female may be pursued into herbage, with surprising mechanical sounds being heard should the lady be unwilling to mate. Yet another big dragonfly, the Emperor, has been in good numbers over the Levels and on Mendip in the past summer; the spectacular and often seemingly tireless males will quickly chase any trespassers, which are normally expelled without a fight.

Many dragonfly species, however, do not behave in any marked territorial manner, with males securing mates without much obvious aggression. Thus, large parties of male Azure Dragonflies will fly in sunshine near a pond and then perch in vegetation to look out for likely females; other species which behave similarly are both the Common Blue and the Blue-tailed Damselflies. However, Beautiful and Banded Demoiselle males will actively guard their shore patches, where females will lay their eggs into secluded vegetation. In contrast, Emerald Damselfly males show little aggression, probably linked with their association with dense water vegetation which must restrict chasing behaviour.

One hawker dragonfly which does not obviously guard a territory is the Migrant Hawker, a late summer insect, and which appeared to have been especially numerous in Somerset during August; doubtless local populations were increased by migratory parties from France. Commonly, groups of Migrant Hawkers of both sexes can be seen circling several metres up in woodland glades or over marshes, sometimes but not always fly-catching and normally non-aggressive towards other dragonflies. In early August, a lot of Migrant Hawkers appeared over Quantock villages and it was common to see up to twenty flying in the sunshine over my own garden. Several neighbours told me of big numbers of dragonflies, almost certainly the same species, seen over their gardens; one reliable witness mentioned at least two hundred of the insects. Swallows tried to snap up some of the dragonflies and I also saw a few Chaffinches, and one Great Tit, chasing them, although unsuccessfully. Strangely, some amphibians, as well as Migrant Hawkers, were reported in big numbers in early August. A farmer told me of hundreds of Common Frogs he had seen in his fields, while it was difficult to stop them coming into his buildings; later, young Common Toads appeared, behaving in the same way. No doubt amphibians had bred well in this area in the past season, in spite of a cold late winter.

Butterflies evidently appreciated the warm summer, with good numbers of several species. Clouded Yellows, as immigrants, had an excellent year; I saw the last one on 15 October in my own garden. Commas, Peacocks and Red Admirals fared well but, in contrast, few Small Tortoiseshells were on the wing.[46] Amongst day-flying moths, I had several sightings of Humming-bird Hawk-moths, often feeding from Valerian flowers; I expect that most of these insects were immigrants, and another of these with big numbers was the Silver-Y moth. I did not find that wasps were a nuisance last autumn when they like to taste sweet items, such as decomposing apples or picnic jam. But Hornets, the

46 A Small Tortoiseshell in August; these colourful butterflies love gardens with plenty of flower beds. Eggs are laid on Stinging Nettles, so there is something to be said for keeping a few wild patches about. Numbers of this butterfly vary a lot in Somerset from year to year.

largest of the British wasps, were plentiful, and active well into late autumn; they are industrious insects, with the workers carrying in insect prey to feed the colony larvae well into darkness on fine, warm evenings. I like to see a few Hornets around as they are such beautiful woodland insects, although I would not relish a sting! Actually a friend was stung by a hornet in the autumn; he said that the immediate effect was no worse than an ordinary wasp sting, but the pain lasted longer.

One feature of last autumn was the good and varied hooting of Tawny Owls at night; often the sounds are made by young birds of the year asserting their possession of territory. I have been told that, in general, the breeding success of owls was poor last season because of prolonged cold in late winter and early spring, so reducing mouse and vole prey. Owls cannot readily locate prey on the woodland floor during heavy rain or gales, as they cannot hear animals moving in the leaf litter; however, I would not have thought that cold, frosty nights would reduce potential prey to any great extent, and we had no continuous snow cover. Anyway, moving to the sea-shore, I was pleased to watch some Curlew feeding on tidal mud flats. I saw one Curlew seize a small frog from a grassy clump and I wondered how the bird, with its long, thin bill, could possibly deal with prey of this shape when, usually, it takes worm-type food. In fact, the frog was skilfully tossed to the centre of the bill and gradually moved to the back; then, with a gulp, the meal was swallowed, as proved by a bulge moving down the neck.

In the autumn, birds seemed to desert our gardens, much to the worry of some kind villagers, who regularly supply seeds or peanuts. I think the explanation is the abundance of food in the woods and hedges; there have been fine crops of Hawthorn and Holly berries, Beech mast, acorns and Sweet Chestnuts. No doubt birds will soon return to garden bird-tables when winter weather really sets in. As well as Hawthorn and Holly, I was pleased to see a good crop of Spindle berries too; at least, Spindle fruit is enjoyed by House Sparrows and Blackbirds, although few other birds get attracted. Spindle fruiting capsules, pink and four-lobed, are beautiful structures and add to the attractiveness of any hedge in late summer. One Quantock bird feature of late summer was the repeated drumming of Great Spotted Woodpeckers. I thought this September drumming rather unusual but, on searching the bird literature, it seems to be quite normal!

Fungal mycelium got well-baked last summer, so I expected good fruiting body crops. Happily, when rain finally arrived, local woods produced a good variety of toadstool and mushroom species. Amongst these, the white Porcelain Fungus, sprouting from damaged Beech wood, has been particularly eye-catching with thin, delicate and slimy caps, so often arranged in artistic groupings, and they are edible too, although very bland in flavour. The Cauliflower Fungus, really looking like a cauliflower too, grows on dead pine stumps and was common last autumn; it is quite edible and I found the flesh to be sweet and nutty. Needless to say, perhaps, Cauliflower Fungi taste better when young. Also good eating are Parasols, quite common on Quantock grassland; additionally, Parasols are very photogenic with their concentric, geometric cap patterns. Yet another common fungus which photographs well is the Sulphur Tuft, clustered on dead tree stumps and with differing shades of yellow and brown. Sulphur Tuft mycelium must break down more dead wood than almost any other fungal species, as it is so widespread right across the northern hemisphere. Of course, there are many other fungi which break down dead wood and these include the small, reddish species which sprout in tufts from fallen trunks. The delicate caps are attractively grooved and a red fluid is exuded if the stem is broken; again, these fungi, when young, make excellent subjects for photography.

The Heron's pectinated claw; the effects of a wet summer; an alpha male stag on the Quantocks. 2007

In late July, through a gap in a reed-bed on the Somerset Levels, I was mystified when I saw a rounded, white patch which was moving from side to side. Adding to the mystery, there were grey stripes to be seen as well and also a leg, or sometimes two, beneath the patch. Of course, what I was watching was the rear end of a preening Grey Heron; the bird was very occupied and evidently unaware of my presence. Grey Herons eat slimy Eels, so preening is of great importance; to help the cleansing process, the birds have tracts of powder-down producing feathers and, in addition, there is a pectinated third claw. So, after dealing with a slimy fish, feathers are dusted with powder-down with slime being removed by the comb claw and, presumably, feather lice can be dealt with in the same way. As well as Herons, Nightjars also have a pectinated claw, used here to comb moth scales from the plumage and mouth bristles.

I expect that fish-eating birds fared reasonably well during the heavy rains of the 2007 summer but small birds, such as leaf-warblers, had trouble in finding sufficient caterpillars to feed their young and I fear that it was the same with larger warblers such as the Blackcap or Garden Warbler. Heavy rain washed caterpillars from the leaves and many nests must have become water-saturated, so reducing nestling insulation; further, many insect species do not fly during dull, stormy weather, so food supply was reduced for Swallows or for fly-catching birds in general. Again, Swifts feed only on insects captured in the air and will rest up in recesses in a near-torpid state during periods of rainy weather. Probably owl nestlings had to make do with a reduced diet too, because the sounds of heavy rain will prevent adult owls hearing mice or voles moving in vegetation. As with butterflies, most moths will not fly during prolonged rain, so I suspect that Nightjars did not find enough food for their young during the nesting season.

Birds such as Spotted Flycatchers, Cuckoos or Willow Warblers have declined alarmingly in the Somerset countryside in the past few years; one can but hope that the 2008 bird-breeding season will be more favourable than that of the past year. However, I have the impression that marsh and lakeside birds had some breeding success, except where nests got flooded out. Reed Warblers certainly had free-flying young in late summer although I did not see any young Sedge Warblers. One family party which I noted in flight over a reed-bed in late July comprised ten Long-tailed Tits. Long-tailed Tits start nesting early, often in March, so a successful brood may well be on the wing by mid-summer; unfortunately, early nests are so often ragged out by Jays or Magpies. In late August, again on the Levels, I saw a small bird emerge from a reed-bed and fly to cling to a dead, upright branch of a willow which had fallen into a lake. The bird was red-brown, plump and had a longish tail which was often held cocked, Wren-like; clearly this was a Cetti's Warbler, a resident, which is far more often heard than seen as it usually stays well-concealed in vegetation. Even so, this bird descended the willow stick head-first until its beak was almost at the water surface and then pecked round to secure some small food items of unknown identity. Amazingly to me, the Cetti's Warbler behaved just like a Nuthatch when descending the stick head-first; Treecreepers only ascend tree trunks and when woodpeckers go down a tree they do so tail-first.

Another unexpected item of bird behaviour was the amount of Chaffinch song on the Quantock Hills during September. Migrants, such as Chiffchaffs or Willow Warblers, often give a few snatches of song in early autumn before they depart, but some of the Chaffinch song was quite persistent and heard well into October; indeed, I made a note for the 2nd of October that dawn Chaffinch song that day reminded me of a March day. On the same day, successive waves of House Martins flew over my garden to the south-west; clearly, the birds were part of a big migratory movement and I expect that re-orientation occurred on reaching the coast. At times, some of the martins would pause, to fly round local woodland while fly-catching; obviously, a lot of flies are necessary as fuel for the long journey ahead.

Dragonflies have not had much sunshine in which to fly and mate this summer but, from time to time, there has been behaviour worth noting. As one example, on an August day on the Levels, I saw both a male and a female Ruddy Darter hovering close to each other in the usual expert fashion;[47] I assumed that the male would soon attempt to grab and join in tandem with the female but, instead, both insects started to bend the hind parts of the abdomen up and down, thus giving the impression of enjoyable aerial dancing! Female dragonflies will bend the rear aspect of the abdomen downwards, so suggesting egg-laying, when they are not in a mating mood but here both sexes were carrying out the movements. What was the explanation? On another occasion, on the Mendips, two or sometimes three male Southern Hawkers flew to chase blown thistle seeds; it was a windy, overcast day with little to see so the observation was especially enjoyable. Southern Hawkers are powerful fliers and I assumed that they were really after a good, meaty meal – how disappointing for them!

Last summer I was hoping to see a Small Red Damselfly as I had heard that one had been authentically recorded by a Priddy Mineries pool in 2006, although it had been assumed that the species had recently become extinct in Somerset. Thus, one July day, I was thrilled to see a

47 A male Ruddy Darter photographed near West Quantoxhead in August. It is smaller than the Common Darter and has a striking blood-red abdomen with a waist, as well as black legs. The female is straw-coloured. Not infrequently, these dragonflies will cross the English Channel as immigrants in summer, to supplement local populations.

small, thin red damsel in flight in the same area; it soon settled on herbage and I was able to confirm that the legs were red, so the insect could not possibly have been a late Large Red Damselfly. This sighting was the first of this species I have seen definitely in Somerset; I got the insect in the viewfinder of my camera but before I had a proper focus it flew off, low down, and got lost in vegetation so no photographic confirmation was obtained – very sad. Still, one dragonfly which was not scarce in Somerset last summer was the Common Darter; in early September, on the Levels, at least one hundred individuals were counted when perched or in the air, while mating pairs were commonplace. Also, at the same location, Ruddy Darters were in good numbers although no Black Darters were seen; however, Black Darters appeared to be thriving on the Mendip Hills in August.**[48]**

Butterflies did not have a good season, with reduced numbers of most species, including the normally abundant Meadow and Hedge Browns, although I believe that some woodland species fared much better.

48 A Black Darter mating pair. Black Darters are not uncommon over boggy parts of Exmoor and the Mendips; unusually, the larvae do not necessarily need open water as they can live in mud, eating soil invertebrates.

Even so, it might have been thought that the heavy summer rainfall would induce a good showing of autumn fungi but this does not seem to have happened; I have not met anyone who has had a proper meal of Field Mushrooms this autumn. Somehow I think that fungal mycelium did not get sufficient midsummer sunshine and baking and, further, the late summer and autumn was very dry. Nevertheless, I did find some worthwhile fungal specimens on Exmoor and one of these had a brown cap with irregular whitish spots. I thought at first that this was a Panther Cap, a really poisonous species, but the spotting was grey rather than pure white so the agaric was a False Panther Cap; this is said to be edible but I did not test the theory! Then, amongst Birches, I saw both the Orange and the Brown Birch Bolete; cap colour differs here but the stalks of both fungi are attractively speckled with dark brown scales. Another pored fungus I found that day was amongst Scots Pines; this was the rather viscid Slippery Jack with large brown caps and yellow pores, and which makes an excellent meal. Moving to Quantock Beech groves, I saw

several clustered growths of the Poached Egg or Porcelain Fungus; this
very slimy white agaric has a beautiful structure and it seems sad that its
life has to be so brief.**[49]** I think it is always exciting if a *Cortinarius*
species is discovered, with rusty gills and a web or partial veil. One
Cortinarius I came across proved to be a Birch-associated species, but I
could not be sure of the identification until spores had been examined
and, of course, a spore print must be taken. Other fungal groups
common over the Quantocks this autumn included puff-balls **[50]** and
Mycena species. Many fallen trunks showed small reddish fungi, helping
to break down dead wood; these fungi show a reddish juice on breaking
the stem. Some local pastures had varied and interesting fungal growths;
certainly I have seen plenty of the hallucinogenic Liberty Caps as well as
different dung fungi, while the small radially-grooved White Cap is
particularly attractive, especially after rain, and may be found in both
spring and autumn.

This year I found the October Red Deer rut on the Quantocks to be as
dramatic as usual. In mid-October I was able to watch, when light
permitted, a very fine stag with, I think, ten antler points who controlled

49 The Poached Egg or Porcelain Fungus is delicate, very slimy and grows on dead Beech. The fungi can be
eaten but I would rather admire them on the tree.

50 This Puff-ball is edible when young but not when it matures and forms spores. The specimen here is sited spectacularly on a dark patch of the woodland floor.

ten hinds, and, in the same area, there was a young stag with much smaller antlers who controlled four hinds. Clearly, the smaller, upstart stag was a real annoyance to the more senior one, and was chased off on many occasions but only to return, although keeping, in the main, a respectful distance. The ornate Red Deer antlers present at the time of the rut are remarkable bony structures, with complexity increasing according to the stag's maturity. Antlers start to grow, after shedding, in March, and are fully developed by July or August, with all this happening on a mainly grass diet too. Somehow I think that Red Deer stags roar best just before dawn when chasing activity is increasing as well; by day, deer will have retreated from the open rutting zone to the cover of woodland, at least in most cases. At dusk, the stag will herd his hinds into an arena, perhaps in a forest clearing or a field, and there they will stay, if undisturbed, until the next day. Should disturbance occur, there is usually a retreat into woodland but there is a risk of hinds getting scattered and, in this case, they have to be rounded up once again. One memory of the dawn deer rut this year on the Quantocks was an occasion one October dawn when Tawny Owl hoots seemed almost to alternate with stag roars, as though bird and mammal were enjoying a duet! Frustratingly, although I had made a sound recording, it was ruined by some unexplained electrical interference and, of course, these unique sound pictures are never repeated. Anyway, by 24 October, what must have been the original stag which was dominant early in the month had increased its female herd from ten to no less than thirty two. I understand that hinds become fertile in their third year, but they are only receptive to the stag's advances for a day or two; it follows that Red Deer males have to work hard to mate successfully with each female in the group in the course of around two weeks. It is no wonder that possessive stags have little or no time for feeding or sleeping at rutting time; no straying can be permitted and, for a hind, the sounds of such powerful roars and loud, expulsive grunts must be really intimidating when close-by. For mating to take place between hind and stag at the correct time everything must depend on scent; it is not surprising that the Red Deer's nose bones and membranes have such a big surface area when compared with those of humans. By the end of October my 'special' stag had departed and the hinds had dispersed; now I must wait until next October for stag belling to recommence, linked with the often spectacular round-up of hinds. The power of a dominant stag's roars and the lack of tolerance for any other mature male in the area surely demonstrates the potency of a Red Deer stag's sex hormones!